THE BASICS OF WRITING

Book 3

Don L. Wulffson

Globe Book Company, Inc.
New York / Cleveland / Toronto

DON WULFFSON teaches English, remedial reading, and creative writing at San Fernando High School in Los Angeles. He graduated from the University of California at Los Angeles, where he later conducted postgraduate research in education.

His awards of merit include the Distinguished Achievement Award from the Educational Press Association of America and the Leather Medal Award for poetry. Mr. Wulffson has been distinguished as an Outstanding Educator in America.

He has written 14 books for young people, 10 learning programs, and more than 300 stories, poems, and plays for a variety of publications, both adult and juvenile.

Consultants:

Dr. Vivian Grano, Ed. D.
Executive Assistant to the Superintendent
The Office of Manhattan High Schools
122 Amsterdam Avenue
New York, New York

Constance Hill
English Department
North Junior High School
Colorado Springs,
Colorado

Editors: Amy Levin and Andrew P. Morris
Photo Editor: Adelaide Garvin Ungerland
Illustrations: Gerald Smith
   The Classroom Cartoon: Created by Robert Guillen; drawn by Gerald Smith
Text Design: Barbara Bert, North 7 Atelier, Ltd.
Cover Art: Gerald Smith
Typesetting: York Graphic Services, Inc.

Photo Acknowledgments: Page 7—United Press International; 37—Frederic Lewis/Harold M. Lambert; 44—United Press International; 98—Movie Still Archives

Other Acknowledgments

Cartoon from *Who Do You Think You Are, Charlie Brown?* by Charles Schulz. Copyright © 1959 United Feature Syndicate, Inc.

"Dreams Can Come True," originally entitled "Dream World," by Don L. Wulffson, from *Read* magazine Teacher's Edition, copyright © 1983 by *Weekly Reader.*—"Infiltration," "Portrait of Death," and "The Dream of Elton John," adapted from "From Super Soft to Superstar: The Elton John Story," by Don L. Wolffson, copyright © 1981 by *Weekly Reader.* All four selections used by permission of *Read* magazine, Xerox Education Publications. This agreement is assignable to any successor organization of Xerox Education Publications.

"Richard Cory" from *Children of the Night* by Edwin Arlington Robinson, courtesy of the publisher, Charles Scribner's Sons.

Second Edition 1987

ISBN: 0-87065-346-6

CONTENTS

1. DAYDREAMING / 2   **Writing:** Daydream Paragraph / 5
   Skill Building: Using Capital Letters / 6

2. STORIES, FROM BEGINNING TO END / 9   **Writing:** Conclusion to a Story / 16
   Skill Building: Pronouns and Case / 17

3. DREAMWORLDS / 21   **Writing:** Descriptive Paragraph / 25
   Skill Building: End-of-Sentence Punctuation / 25

4. SUMMARIZING / 28   **Writing:** Summary Paragraph / 34
   Skill Building: Homophones / 34

5. IT'S NEWS TO ME / 37   **Writing:** News Story / 42
   Skill Building: Sentence Fragments / 43

6. PLAYFUL CONVERSATIONS / 46   **Writing:** Short Play / 53
   Skill Building: Subject-Verb Agreement / 54

7. FRIENDLY PERSUASION / 57   **Writing:** Letter of Persuasion / 62
   Skill Building: Avoiding Run-Ons / 63

8. WHAT'S THE POINT? / 65   **Writing:** Story with a Theme / 70
   Skill Building: Punctuation / 70

9. COMIC RELIEF / 72   **Writing:** Your Cartoon / 77
   Skill Building: The Comma / 78

10. PARTNER STORIES / 81   **Writing:** A Partner Story / 86
    Skill Building: The Semicolon / 86

11. I MEAN BUSINESS / 89   **Writing:** A Business Letter / 95
    Skill Building: The Colon / 95

12. HOLLYWOOD—SUMMING UP / 98   **Writing:** A Movie Summary / 103
    Skill Building: Parentheses / 103

13. OBJECTIVE POETRY / 105   **Writing:** Objective Poems / 110
    Skill Building: The Hyphen / 111

14. THE THINGS PEOPLE SAY / 114   **Writing:** A Compositon / 118
    Skill Building: Quotation Marks / 119

15. THE FICTIONAL TWIST / 121   **Writing:** A Story / 126
    Skill Building: Quotation Marks in a Story / 126

16. THE INTEPRETIVE ESSAY / 129   **Writing:** An Interpretive Essay / 134
    Skill Building: Punctuation Review / 135

17. IN A WORD: WRITING / 137   Review and Application / 140
    Writing: Your Choice / 142

1 DAYDREAMING

Most people have daydreams. They daydream about something they would like to have happen.

We asked some students in New England to write about their daydreams. The following cartoons tell what they wrote. Read the daydreams. You may even recognize one of your own.

THINKING ABOUT WHAT YOU HAVE READ

Answer in complete sentences.

1. It is not easy to make our dreams come true. Which of the daydreams do you think would be hardest to achieve? Explain.

_____

_____

_____

_____

2. Which daydream is the most realistic? Which do you think would be easiest to achieve? Explain your answer.

_____

_____

_____

_____

3. Which of the daydreams is most like one you may have had? Explain.

_____

_____

_____

4. Many people have accomplished great things. Their accomplishments probably began as daydreams. Do you agree? Explain.

_____

_____

_____

_____

5. Why, in your opinion, do people daydream?

_____

_____

_____

THINKING ABOUT WRITING

From General To Specific

When we write, we usually start with a general statement and then add details. That is, the first, or **topic, sentence** explains our general idea. The sentences that follow support or explain the opening sentence.

Read the following paragraph.

The one thing I have always wanted to be is a soldier. It doesn't matter if it is in the army, the navy, or the marines. It doesn't matter to me if I serve as an officer or I just enlist. To serve my country as a soldier would be a dream come true. That is really all I want.

The first sentence is the topic sentence. It makes a general statement. The topic sentence states the idea that the writer wants to be a soldier. The other sentences support or expand this idea. They add information about the topic sentence.

Read each group of sentences. Underline the statement that could be the topic sentence—the one that is most general and that states the broadest idea. Then number the sentences in the order in which they would make a logical paragraph. One sentence has been numbered for you.

1. ___3___ **a.** Second, I will pass laws to help the poor.

   _____ **b.** The first thing I will do is to work for peace in the world.

   _____ **c.** Someday I will be the leader of my country.

   _____ **d.** Third, I will pass laws that will help get rid of the pollution in our environment.

2. _____ **a.** Four years ago she began to train with the coach at school.

   _____ **b.** This year she won more races than anyone in the state.

   _____ **c.** My dream is for my sister to win an Olympic medal for running.

   _____ **d.** Since then she has been training every day for the Oympics.

4

Getting Ready to Write

Soon you will write about a daydream of your own. The following activities will help you get ready to write.

I.

Below are several things people often daydream about. Circle the *one* that most appeals to you. Or, in the blank, write a daydream topic of your own.

becoming a professional athlete   traveling to far-off places   owning a business

becoming an actor   becoming a writer   becoming a doctor or a lawyer

being a hero   owning a car   becoming a famous singer or musician

inventing something   becoming rich   being elected to a political office

doing something nice for someone you care about   living in another place

_____

II.

Briefly describe some of the things you would have to do in order to make your dream come true. What obstacles would you have to overcome?

_____

_____

_____

III.

Explain how you would feel if your dream came true. How would your life change?

_____

_____

_____

Daydream Paragraph

Now it's time to put your daydream into writing. On a separate sheet of paper, describe your dream. Remember to begin with a general statement. Then add details. Use your answers to "Getting Ready to Write" (above) to help you.

SKILL BUILDING

Using Capital Letters

Review and study the following rules of capitalization. Then do the activity.

> You should capitalize . . .
> 1. the first word of every sentence.
> 2. the names of people (Ms. Paula Sheldon).
> 3. the pronoun I.
> 4. the names of days, months, and holidays. (This year Valentine's Day, February 14, falls on a Tuesday.)
> 5. the names of streets (West Lennox Avenue).
> 6. the names of countries, states, cities, and rivers. (St. Louis, Missouri, is on the Mississippi River.)
> 7. the titles of books, magazines, plays, and movies (The Adventures of Huckleberry Finn, 2001: A Space Odyssey).
> 8. the names of societies, clubs, churches, schools, hospitals, and colleges (Hobart High School, Wilderness Society, Drama Club).

None of the words in the following selection has been capitalized. Read the selection carefully. Then add capital letters where they are needed. Two letters have been added for you.

the dream of elton john

one of the interesting things about elton john is that his name was not always elton john. the name he was given at birth was reginald dwight.

as a boy, reginald was overweight and very shy. only rarely did he venture outside his home in london. most of his time was spent indoors, banging out songs on a piano.

young reginald was determined to be a success in the world of music; that was his dream. he wanted to be another elvis presley, the king of rock and roll in the 1950s. reginald attended london's royal academy of music. there he took courses in composition, music history, and harmonics.

reginald's first musical break came when he joined bluesology, a backup

6

group for a british rock singer named long john baldry. but being on stage was not easy for reginald, who was still overweight and very shy.

when bluesology stopped performing rock and roll and switched to ballads, reginald left the group and started looking for another job. after an audition at a music company, reginald just happened to read some lyrics submitted to the company by an unknown songwriter named bernie taupin. reginald was impressed. he called taupin, and the two decided to become a team. for the next 18 months they worked together writing song after song.

during this period, reginald dwight became a new person. he went on a diet and lost 50 pounds. then he changed his name. from bluesology members elton dean and john baldry, he created the name elton john.

in 1969 elton john cut his first single record and his first album. neither sold well. in 1970 he cut another album—entitled *elton john*—which shot up to the top ten in the united states. the albums *captain fantastic, brown dirt cowboy,* and *blue moves* followed in quick succession. all were big hits.

he started out as reginald dwight, a roly-poly shy kid. but he was a kid with a dream. today he's elton john, and he's a star and a success.

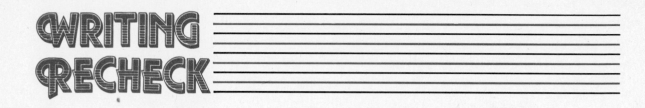

THINKING ABOUT WRITING

1. Does the daydream you described on your paper begin with a general statement that serves as a topic sentence? If not, rewrite your first sentence so that it is a good general introduction to the paragraph. Rewrite the sentence on the lines below.

_____

_____

2. Do the other sentences add specific details that explain and support the opening sentence? If not, on the lines below, rewrite your entire paragraph, adding supporting details. Make sure the details follow in a logical order.

_____

_____

_____

_____

_____

_____

_____

_____

_____

_____

SKILL BUILDING

3. Review the rules of capitalization on page 6. Then carefully check the capitalization in your daydream paragraph. Correct any errors you find.

STORIES, FROM BEGINNING TO END

When you read a story, you want to see how it ends. You want to know how everything works out. Of course, in any story, things can work out in a number of different ways.

Read "Education Day." Then read the three possible endings. Think about which ending is best. Decide which one best fulfills your expectations for the story.

Education Day

For Terry Zaonz, August 12, 2947, was a special day. It was his 18th birthday. And that meant it was Education Day, just as it was for every new 18-year-old on Earth.

During the morning Terry dawdled, trying to fight the nervousness—the fear—he felt. His parents kept telling him not to worry, to relax. But their assurances did no good. With a lump in his throat he idled about, one eye on the clock, unable to do anything in particular.

And then his father said it: "Time to go, son."

"Yes, sir," answered Terry.

Terry hugged his father, then his mother. He stepped into the beam-transporter. Trying to look brave, he watched as his father tapped in the code destination for the Nevada Education Day building. Terry managed a faint smile, took a deep breath, and pushed the flight button.

One moment—and 400 miles later—he found himself inside the plastic-dome complex. "Follow the red line," said a voice, over the star-sound system. Dutifully, in step with scores of other 18-year-olds, Terry followed the line into the Education Room. An attendant guided him toward an Education Booth and put an Education Helmet on his head.

Now study the three possible endings to the story.

1. The doors to the booth closed. Gradually, Terry became aware of a funny sensation in his head. It wasn't a bad feeling, just a funny one. He felt his mind filling with something. It was knowledge. He began to know all about math and science and history. Then he seemed to know everything there was to know. Suddenly the strange sensation was over, and the doors to the booth opened. Education Day had ended, and Terry knew everything. He even knew that long before his time, people spent their whole lives trying to learn everything—and never could. Education Day turned out to be not so bad after all.

2. "What am I going to become?" Terry asked the attendant. "I want to be a musician or a . . ."

"You know the rules! No questions!" snapped the man.

The door to the booth slammed shut. Suddenly Terry felt a painful whirring sensation inside his head. Then his eyes went blank.

He woke up in the recovery room. A woman handed him a glass of water. "Congratulations, you're now educated," she said. "You're a mathematician."

Terry jerked to a sitting position. "A mathematician?" he cried. "But I wanted to become a painter or a musician. I wanted . . ."

"Your feelings don't count. You know the rules. The state gives you your education; the state decides what you will be."

Terry shook his head. "But it's not fair," he cried.

"You will be given your work orders in the morning." The woman turned and walked out.

Terry took a sip of water. "It's not fair," he said to no one. "It's not fair."

3. For a long time Terry just stood in the booth. Then suddenly he felt a buzzing in his head. After that, he heard a voice. The voice said, "We are sorry, but you are not the right kind of person. You do not deserve an education. This has been decided by our brain scanner. Please leave the booth."

With tears in his eyes, Terry took off the Education Helmet. He opened the doors of the booth and headed toward the nearest beam-transporter.

THINKING ABOUT WHAT YOU HAVE READ

Answer in complete sentences.

1. What did Education Day turn out to be in ending number 1? What happened on that day to Terry?

_____

_____

_____

2. What happened in ending number 2? Why did Terry say, "It's not fair"?

_____

_____

_____

3. What was the purpose of Education Day in ending number 3? Could this too be considered unfair?

_____

_____

_____

4. Do you think that all of the endings work well with the story? Do you personally like one of the endings better than the others? Explain.

_____

_____

_____

_____

5. What are some of the other possible ways this story might have ended? Describe some of your ideas.

_____

_____

_____

_____

THINKING ABOUT WRITING

Conflict and Climax

I.

Some sort of **conflict** or struggle is at the center of most stories. For example, imagine a story about a girl floating on a log surrounded by sharks. You want to know how this conflict ends—whether the girl survives. That is what makes the story suspenseful and exciting.

There are seven basic types of story conflicts.

1. *People against people*—An example would be a story about an unknown boxer fighting the world champion.

2. *People against nature*—An example would be a story about a pioneer family that gets lost in the snow. The family struggles to survive.

3. *People against society*—An example would be a story about a person who works to change laws that are unfair to elderly people.

4. *People against machines*—An example would be a story about a computer that learns to think on its own. The machine starts giving wrong answers on purpose to hurt people.

5. *People at odds with themselves (mental conflict)*—An example would be a story about someone who has cheated on a test. The person struggles to decide whether to tell the truth or to let someone else be wrongfully punished.

6. *People against the supernatural*—An example would be a story about a ghost that wants revenge.

7. *People against the unknown*—An example would be a story about a woman exploring an underwater cave.

In the story "Education Day" the main character, Terry Zaonz, is involved in conflict. Answer the following questions about conflict in the story.

1. One type of conflict is with the unknown. When does Terry struggle with the unknown? Where is this struggle described in the story?

   _____

   _____

   _____

2. "Education Day" is a story with conflict between people and society. How is this conflict presented? Explain.

   _____

   _____

   _____

3. Suppose on Education Day Terry had to choose what he would do for the rest of his life. What type of conflict would he have had? Explain.

   _____

   _____

   _____

   _____

II.

The **climax** of a story is the moment when the conflict is resolved. It is the turning point, the moment in which all becomes clear to the reader.

The following story is complete—except for the climax. Read the story. Then answer the questions on a separate sheet of paper.

The Portrait

Putnam knew now what he must do.

A brush clutched in one hand, he sat fixed, immobile. Hypnotically he stared at the empty canvas before him. His mind was turned inward on the past.

Putnam thought back to all that had happened. His soul cried out at the cruel, impossible trick that life had played on him. The talent to paint was the gift that life had bestowed upon him. And in that gift lay the curse.

He had fought the curse for so long, even before he was fully aware of it.

When he was young, he had avoided doing portraits, contenting himself with seascapes and landscapes. But he had always known that his talent lay elsewhere. His talent lay in the painting of portraits.

Father Benson had been the first to come to him. He had begged to have his portrait done. Reluctantly, Putnam had agreed. For weeks he labored on the picture. And two days after it was finished, Father Benson had died.

For many months Putnam did not paint another portrait. Then he took a second client. She was a small woman, an innkeeper. She sat patiently and proudly as her picture was painted. Then, suddenly and unexpectedly, two days later, she died.

It was just coincidence, Putnam had told himself. And as if to prove this, he had done yet another portrait. This man also died. A shadow of grief settled over Putnam's soul. Never again would he paint a portrait.

For seven years he kept his vow. Then he met Elizabeth. They had become engaged. He told her of the curse, but she had laughed. She begged him to do her portrait. She begged him to prove that the curse was, as she put it, "so silly and impossible."

And he had done it. He had painted the woman he loved. He had put her into her grave.

And now, sitting alone in his studio, Putnam knew what he must do. Tears rolling down his face, he put his memories behind him. He set his mind to the task at hand. Staring at the blank canvas as though it were a mirror, he raised his brush and began to paint a portrait of _____.

Follow the directions for each item. Where necessary, write your answers on a separate sheet of paper.

1. Below are several possible endings for the story. Decide which one would make the best climax. Then write it in the blank at the end of the story.

   a. death **d.** himself

   b. Elizabeth **e.** Father Benson

   c. the ocean **f.** life

2. Give reasons for your answer to number 1. Tell why the ending you chose makes the most effective climax.

3. In "The Portrait," one type of conflict is with the supernatural. Explain how this conflict is illustrated in the story.

4. The story also illustrates mental conflict. How does this conflict affect what happens in the story?

5. The climax of a story resolves the conflicts. That is, one force or the other in each conflict triumphs. In "The Portrait," how is the conflict with the supernatural resolved? Which side wins?

6. How is the mental conflict resolved? What decision does Putnam make?

14

Getting Ready to Write

Soon you will write the ending to a story. The following exercise will help you get ready to write.

1. Read the first four paragraphs of the story "Winner Takes All," below.

2. Do you think a tie would be a good ending to the story? Explain.

   _____

   _____

3. If one leader lost, what might be the reaction of the people who support him? Explain.

   _____

   _____

4. If one side accused the other of cheating, what might happen?

   _____

   _____

5. What are some of the other ways the story might end? Write some of your ideas.

   _____

   _____

Now read the entire story. Then complete the writing assignment on page 16.

Winner Takes All

International Stadium was buzzing with incredible tension and excitement. Over one-hundred thousand people were packed in the stands. Some waved small Landian flags, others the flag of Mountainia. Dozens of TV cameras relayed the scene to viewers around the world.

An announcer strode to the center of the arena floor. "Ladies and gentlemen," he said, his voice booming over the loudspeakers. "Today is the day we have all waited for, the day that Mountainia and Landia settle their differences!"

The spectators cheered—roared their approval.

"Today the president of Landia and the premier of Mountainia will meet in a contest of arm wrestling. To the winner goes the world!"

Another roar of approval became an ecstatic cheer as the Landian president, under heavy guard, entered the arena from the one tunnel. Thousands of flags, signs, and banners were waved, turning the stadium into a rippling rainbow. An instant later, from the other tunnel, the premier of Mountainia made his entrance; Mountainian rooters jumped to their feet, cheering, clapping, waving their own banners and flags.

The two contestants met in the center of the arena. The crowd was quiet as the men shook hands and sat down across from each other at a stainless-steel table. Judges, commentators, and government officials went to their assigned stations.

A referee made his way to the table. He looked at the premier, then at the president. He pulled down an overhead microphone. His voice reverberating in the stadium, he said, "Good afternoon, gentlemen. You know the rules, I am quite sure. You understand that once the contest concludes, both sides agree to destroy or discard all weapons, and the winner will peacefully take control of this planet."

"Agreed," said the premier, leaning toward the microphone.

"Yes, agreed," said the president.

"Then let us begin."

The premier and the president eyed one another. They put their right elbows on the table; their right hands gripped at the thumb. A nervous silence fell over the crowd. TV cameras moved in closer to the contestants.

The referee put his hand on the two clenched fists. "Begin!" he ordered.

CWRITING

Conclusion to a Story

On a separate sheet of paper, write what you think is a good and exciting ending to the story "Winner Takes All." Use your answers to "Getting Ready to Write" (page 15) to help you.

SKILL BUILDING

Pronouns and Case

A **pronoun** is a word used in place of a noun. Notice how pronouns take the place of nouns in the following sentences.

(nouns):   *Andy* met *the girls* at the beach.
(pronouns):   *He* met *them* at the beach.

In the maze that follows, find and circle all the pronouns listed below. Note that pronouns go across, down, and diagonally. When you find a word in the puzzle, cross it off the list. The pronoun *he* is circled and crossed out as an example.

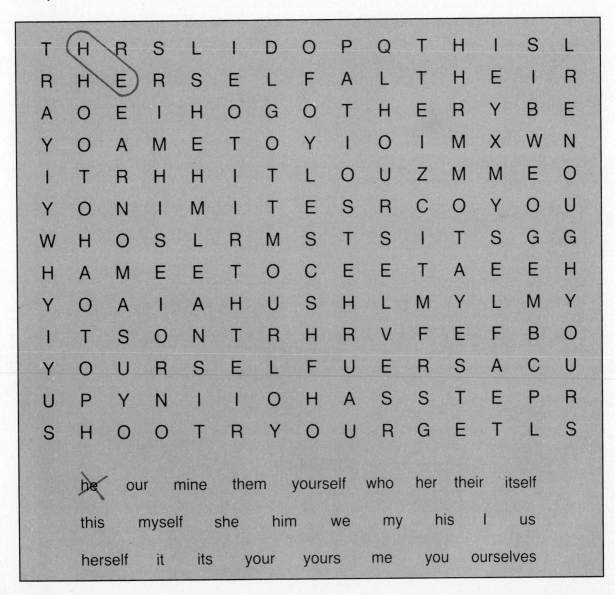

Pronouns have different forms, depending on how they are used in a sentence. The different forms are called *cases*. Pronouns have three different cases:

SUBJECT (NOMINATIVE) CASE		OBJECT (OBJECTIVE) CASE		OWNERSHIP (POSSESSIVE) CASE	
Singular	*Plural*	*Singular*	*Plural*	*Singular*	*Plural*
I	we	me	us	my, mine	our, ours
you	you	you	you	your, yours	your, yours
he, she, it	they	him, her, it	them	his, her, hers, its	their, theirs

A pronoun is in the subject (nominative) case when it can be used as the subject of a sentence.

> **EXAMPLES:** <u>I</u> helped that man.
> <u>We</u> helped that man.

A pronoun is in the object (objective) case when it can be used as the object of a verb or a preposition.

> **EXAMPLES:** The dog chased <u>me</u>.
> Throw the ball to <u>her</u>.

A pronoun is in the ownership (possessive) case when it shows possession. It is used in place of a possessive noun.

> **EXAMPLES:** Mike ate <u>his</u> sandwich.
> Mom likes <u>their</u> house.

Trying to decide which pronoun case to use can be difficult. That is, pronoun case can cause problems. And the following story is full of such problems. Many pronouns are in the wrong case.

Change each incorrect pronoun to the right case. Cross it out and write the pronoun that is correct. Refer to the list of pronouns and the example sentences above, if you need help. The first change has been made as an example.

Infiltration

Vice-President Sheila Dobler sat quietly in the corridor, waiting to be called. Across the corridor, in a closed and silent room, the president lay dying, a small army of doctors at ~~him~~ *his* side.

The doctors had not explained the sudden failing of President Portman's health. However, at a later date, when necessary, they would provide expert opinions guaranteed to satisfy the public mind.

When death came, as it promised soon to do, Sheila Dobler would, quite suddenly, be thrust into the spotlight as the new leader of a great and troubled nation. The prospect neither pleased nor disturbed she.

The minutes dragged by. Suddenly, the door across the corridor opened, and three doctors emerged.

"The president wishes to see you," announced a white-clad figure, pointing toward the door.

"Us will want to be alone," Dobler explained, edging past the doctors. Shutting the door quietly behind she, her entered the room and found her way to a chair at the president's side.

The president's head moved weakly on the pillow. Him eyes came to rest on Dobler's face.

"You'll soon be filling me shoes," said the president.

"You're going to be fine. You're . . ."

With a faint smile on him lips, the president continued.

"And I think you know what it is us must speak about. We nation has been infiltrated, not by people but by . . ."

"By machines, humanoids," said Dobler, finishing the sentence. "Me find it hard to believe."

"You'd better start believing it," said the president. Our latest reports indicate they are indistinguishable from human beings. And them are infiltrating every area of ours nation's life—business, government, even the military. Them are programmed to destroy this country—and deliver it on a platter to us enemies."

The president coughed, exhausted by what him was saying, what he was thinking.

"You're the one person who can stop it," said the president, closing he eyes, drifting on the edge of consciousness.

Vice-President Sheila Dobler looked calmly down at the dying man. Her felt no pity, and never had during she 12 years of existence, for she was not programmed to do so. Her had been designed to think, not feel—and she thinking was very precise, very accurate. And right now her was thinking about the first steps she would take as the country's next—and unique—president.

THINKING ABOUT WRITING

1. Examine the ending you wrote to "Winner Takes All." When does the moment of climax take place? That is, at what point do you show your reader the outcome of the contest between the president and the premier?

    _____

    _____

    _____

2. Examine the climax you wrote. Does it arrive too fast? Did you let the excitement in the story build, or did you simply rush to bring the story to an end? Explain below. (If the ending seems rushed, you will probably want to rewrite it on your paper.)

    _____

    _____

    _____

3. What conflicts do you find in "Winner Takes All"? Consider both the beginning and your ending in answering this question. Describe these conflicts below.

    _____

    _____

    _____

SKILL BUILDING

4. Reread your ending. Are there any errors in capitalization or in pronoun case? Correct any errors you find.

3

DREAMWORLDS

People spend about a third of their lives sleeping. This means that a person who is fifteen years old has slept a total of about five years! For a large part of the time that we are asleep, strange stories and fantasies—dreams—are unfolding inside our heads.

A group of students in Seattle, Washington, was asked to record their dreams. Some of the dreams are scary. Some are pleasant. All are a bit strange.

Once I had a great dream. I dreamed I was in an old house with long hallways. Instead of walking through the hallways, I flew! I had my arms spread out. I just glided along a few feet above the floor. It was the greatest feeling in the world.

Mary Ling

A few nights ago I had a very weird dream. In the dream, I was looking out a window at my dog. All of a sudden my dog walked through the window. But the window didn't break! At the same time, my dog divided into two parts. The front part of him walked into the house. The back part of him was still outside.

James Lee Walker

Once I dreamed I was like a fish. I was swimming down deep in the ocean. It was very cool, and I was having a great time. The most amazing thing of all was that I could breathe underwater. I didn't have any scuba gear or anything, but I could still breathe.

Linda Pinelli

THINKING ABOUT WHAT YOU HAVE READ

Answer in complete sentences.

1. Which of the dreams do you think is the most frightening? Explain.

_____

_____

2. Which of the dreams seems to be the most pleasant and enjoyable? Explain.

_____

_____

3. Have you ever had a dream like any of those described on page 21? If so, describe your dream. Tell how it is similar to the writer's dream.

_____

_____

4. As you know, a story usually has a conflict that is resolved in the climax, or the ending. Why would this format not always work for writing about dreams?

_____

_____

THINKING ABOUT WRITING

Word Choice and Sequence—Putting the Two Together

Strange things can happen in dreams. You may feel that you are flying or falling from a great height. Objects may seem to move all by themselves or change their size, shape, or color. Sometimes it's hard to tell exactly what *is* going on in a dream.

That is why it is important to choose words carefully. For example, a student wrote the following sentence about a dream she had.

I seemed to be standing at the top of a straight hill.

She realized that the word *straight* was a poor choice. Even in dreams, hills aren't usually thought of as being *straight.* So she erased *straight* and used the word *steep* instead.

I seemed to be standing at the top of a steep hill.

I.

Some poor word choices are underlined in the following dream description. First, read the entire dream. Then, in the numbered blanks after it, write a better word to replace each underlined word in the dream.

EXAMPLE: I opened my eyes, and I thought I had been dreaming.

1.   *realized*

I dreamed I was running down a mountainside in a humorous little train on tracks. Back of me
           (1)   (2)   (3)

was another train, and within it was an angry-looking dude. I stood on the gas pedal, and my train
           (4)   (5)   (6)

quickly went faster. It went so fast that it fell off the tracks and shot out into air. My train had
(7)   (8)   (9)

become a rocket ship, moving me to safety.
           (10)

1. _____   6. _____

2. _____   7. _____

3. _____   8. _____

4. _____   9. _____

5. _____   10. _____

Dreams often seem to have a strange **sequence,** or order. When you write about them, you have to arrange what happens in a logical order. The reader's job is made much easier when you sort out the beginning, middle, and end.
  Notice what happened when a student named Anthony Parks wrote about one of his dreams.

It was raining. I couldn't tell where the rain was coming from. I was the only one who got wet. They stared at me when I opened an umbrella. I forgot to say that I was on a busy street with lots of people around. It was a sunny day.

When Anthony rewrote his description, he moved the details he had forgotten to the beginning of the paragraph. By telling first things first, Anthony made the order of his dream clearer. His rewritten description is on page 24.

It was a sunny day. I was on a busy street with lots of people around. Then it started raining. I couldn't tell where the rain was coming from. I was the only one who got wet. Everyone stared at me when I opened up an umbrella.

II.

The following dream is in a nightmare form! The sentences are in the wrong order. Show the correct order of the sentences by matching their letters with the numbers after the description. One letter has been matched with its correct number.

(a) I heard people's voices calling to me from the cage. (b) But when I got to the top of the ladder and looked in the cage, I found that all the people were gone! (c) Once I dreamed I was walking through a dark valley. (d) I found a ladder and climbed up to the cage. (e) In the valley there was a wooden cage on top of poles.

1. __C__   2. _____   3. _____   4. _____   5. _____

III.

Now put together what you've learned about word choice and logical order. First, show the correct order of the following sentences, as you did for Part II. Then replace the underlined words with better choices. Cross out each underlined word and write your new word (or words) above it.

(a) I just stood there and <u>disbelieved</u> how there could be another ocean on top of the cliff. (b) A few weeks ago, I had a dream that I was at the beach. (c) To get away, I <u>scampered</u> up a cliff behind the beach. (d) Suddenly a huge wave started coming at me. (e) I saw another ocean! (f) When I got to the top of the cliff, I saw something <u>unreal</u>.

1. _____   2. _____   3. _____   4. _____   5. _____   6. _____

Getting Ready to Write

In the writing assignment for this lesson, you will be asked to describe one of your dreams. Are you good at remembering your dreams when you wake up? It isn't always easy! The following activities may help to bring some to mind.

I.

Listed at the top of page 25 is a number of subjects about which people sometimes dream. Underline those you have dreamed about at one time or another. You may add to the list by writing on the line provided.

being chased   getting something you want   looking for something   eating

flying   water   giving a speech   being lost   animals   being in a strange place

seeing and talking to a person you knew long ago   falling   reliving an event

sports   a scary movie or story   _____

II.

Now look over the items you chose for Part I. Circle the *one* that brings the most interesting of your dreams to mind.

Descriptive Paragraph

On a separate sheet of paper, write a paragraph describing one of your dreams. Use your answers to "Getting Ready to Write" (above) to help you get started.

SKILL BUILDING

End-of-Sentence Punctuation

There are three end-of-sentence punctuation marks—the question mark, the exclamation point, and the period.
    The question mark (**?**) shows that something is being asked. Some questions begin with an interrogative such as *who, what, why, when, how, which,* and *where.*

EXAMPLE: <u>Who</u> was that**?** <u>What</u> did he want**?**

Other questions begin with a verb.

EXAMPLE: <u>Is</u> he cold**?** <u>Will</u> you ask him**?**

The exclamation point (**!**) can be used to show surprise, anger, or excitement.

EXAMPLE: (surprise):   I can't believe it!
(anger):   I'm sick of this!
(excitement): That's great!

The exclamation point follows exclamations and usually follows commands.

> **EXAMPLE:** (command): Leave this room immediately!
> (exclamation): Ouch! Wow!

The period **(.)** is used to end all other sentences.

Pictured below is a group of "dream creatures." There is no end-of-sentence punctuation in what they are saying. At the end of each sentence place a **?** or a **!** or just a **.** .

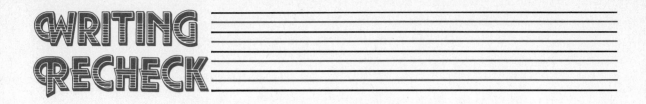

THINKING ABOUT WRITING

1. Examine the paragraph you wrote. Did you choose your words carefully? Cross out any poor word choices. Write a better word to replace each one.

2. Is the description of your dream written in a logical order? If not, on the lines below, rearrange the sentences in a logical sequence.

_____

_____

_____

_____

_____

_____

_____

_____

_____

SKILL BUILDING

3. Check the end-of-sentence punctuation in your paragraph. Are there any errors or omissions? Correct any mistakes you find.

4. Reread your paragraph. Correct any errors you find in capitalization or pronoun case.

SUMMARIZING

Two friends read an interesting news article. Each summarized the story. Read the summaries below. Which one does the best job of telling you what the story was about?

Now read the original news article.

The city council of Harbor Springs, Michigan, passed a really ridiculous law. The law lowered the minimum age for cab drivers from 21 to 18. No one in the town could understand why the council bothered to do this. You see, there aren't any taxis in Harbor Springs!

The age for cab drivers used to be 21. A law was passed. Younger people would be able to drive cabs, which is good, even if there aren't any. The point is, there would have to be a reason for a law if that law is going to be passed. See what I mean?

LAW HAS TOWN UPSET

Harbor Springs, Michigan—The city council voted today to lower the minimum age for cab drivers. The minimum age was dropped from 21 to 18.

Many people are upset about the law. But they're not upset because younger people will be able to drive taxis.

"It's the silliest thing I've ever heard of," said one man. "The law just doesn't make any sense."

And he's right. The law doesn't make any sense. You see, there aren't any taxis in Harbor Springs.

THINKING ABOUT WHAT YOU HAVE READ

Answer in complete sentences.

1. Which of the summaries begins with a topic sentence—a sentence that clearly introduces what the summary is about? On page 28, put a ✔ next to the person (Joe or Bob) whose summary begins with a topic sentence. Then write the sentence below.

   _____

   _____

   _____

2. Which summary tells things in the order in which they happened, and in an order you can follow?

   _____

   _____

   _____

3. Joe's summary contains a lot of wasted words. It includes comments that do not clarify the article. Underline any sentences or phrases you feel are unnecessary.

4. Bob's summary ends with these words: "You see, there aren't any taxis in Harbor Springs." Why did he leave this important information until the end?

   _____

   _____

   _____

   _____

5. When Joe says, "there aren't any," is it clear what he is referring to? Does he effectively get across the main point of the news story? Explain.

   _____

   _____

   _____

   _____

THINKING ABOUT WRITING

The Summary Paragraph

Writers often use what is called a three-sentence paragraph. The three-sentence paragraph has four sentences. It has a topic sentence followed by three supporting sentences. The purpose of the topic sentence is to tell what the rest of the paragraph is about.

The three-sentence paragraph structure makes for an informative, well-organized summary paragraph.

Read the news article. Then complete the activity that follows.

WERE PEOPLE ON EARTH BEFORE PEOPLE WERE ON EARTH?

Antelope Springs, Utah—Scientists reported recently that they had found some *very* old sandal prints. The fossilized prints were tested and found to be about 700 million years old.

But according to experts, humans have been on Earth for only about two million years.

This means that someone may have been walking around in sandals about 698 million years before people were supposed to have been here.

When asked about the prints, one scientist said, "The prints show only one thing. They show how little we know about life on this planet."

I.

Follow the directions for each item.

1. Following is a summary of the above news story. From the choices at the right, pick the best topic sentence for the summary paragraph. Then write it on the lines provided.

_____

_____

The prints were tested and found to be about 700 million years old. People, however, are believed to have been on Earth for only two million years. This discovery has caused the scientists to wonder if people were actually on Earth long before then.

1. Humans have been on earth for only about two million years.

2. No one knows when people first came to be on this planet.

3. Some scientists found sandal prints.

4. Scientists have discovered some very strange sandal prints.

2. Below, briefly explain why you chose that topic sentence. Compare it with those you did not think were as good.

_____

_____

_____

_____

_____

_____

Read the following news item before moving on.

CAN OF FOOT POWDER ELECTED MAYOR OF TOWN IN ECUADOR

Ecuador—The town of Picoaza has a big problem. A foot powder named Pulvapies was elected its new mayor.

A foot powder company decided to make the most out of upcoming elections. It ran ads that promoted their product as if it were a person running for office. The ads were the same size and color as real ballots. Across the top were the words, ''Vote for Pulvapies.''

When the votes were counted, Pulvapies had won by a landslide. There is a big argument now about whether the foot powder should take office.

II.

Below is a summary of the news item about the foot powder. The paragraph has a topic sentence and three supporting sentences. But there are a lot of other sentences thrown in as well. These sentences weaken, rather than improve, the paragraph.

Read the summary carefully. Then cross out the unnecessary sentences. There are five sentences to be crossed out.

It happened in Ecuador. A town in Ecuador actually elected a foot powder as mayor! That was the outcome when the votes were counted. The whole thing began when a company ran ads that promoted its product, Pulvapies foot powder, as if it were a person running for office. It was a terribly stupid idea. The ads were printed to look like official ballots. They were just exactly the same in every way. This confused voters so much that they actually ended up electing the foot powder as mayor. Something like this, as far as I know, has never happened before.

Combining Your Ideas

A summary should be brief. Ideas have to be brought together in such a way that you make your point quickly and with no wasted words.

Short, choppy sentences can get in the way of good writing. But the problem can easily be corrected by combining two or more choppy sentences into a longer, more effective sentence.

EXAMPLE:

(choppy sentences):   Author E. V. Wright wrote a novel. He wrote it in 1939. It has 50,000 words. The novel does not have the letter *E* in it.

(combined):   In 1939 author E. V. Wright wrote a 50,000-word novel in which the letter *E* does not appear.

Rewrite each group of choppy sentences into a single sentence. Make whatever changes in wording are necessary.

1. Sometimes in Siberia it gets very cold. It gets so cold your breath freezes. Your breath falls to the ground like a handful of crystals.

   _____

   _____

   _____

   _____

2. Scientists said something. They said that each of our days at present is longer. It is six times longer than when the earth was first formed.

   _____

   _____

   _____

   _____

3. In 1971 a scuba diver found a dinner plate. It was on the bottom of the ocean. The plate had probably belonged to Christopher Columbus.

   _____

   _____

   _____

   _____

4. In June of 1959, players on a basketball team got angry. They got very angry at the officials. They began shooting baskets for the other team!

_____

_____

_____

_____

5. A doctor once proclaimed something. It was in 1923. The doctor was French. He said people could "see through their skin."

_____

_____

_____

_____

Getting Ready to Write

Soon you will be writing a summary of the following news story. Read it carefully. Then complete the activities that follow.

BURGLAR MAKES A BOO-BOO

Bisbee, Arizona—A burglar broke into the office of a justice of the peace Thursday. He stole a tape recorder, an adding machine, and other items.

The burglar, however, made one small mistake.

During the robbery he dropped his wallet. The wallet, which contained a driver's license and other ID, was found by police.

Yesterday, police drove to the home of Wayne M. Loper, 30. They happily returned Mr. Loper's wallet to him and then arrested him for robbery.

Answer the following questions on the lines provided.

1. List the events reported in the news article. Write them in the order in which they happened.

_____

_____

_____

_____

_____

2. Go back and put a ✔ next to those events listed in question 1 that you consider most important.

3. Write a topic sentence for a summary of the article. The sentence should be general. It should also be an introduction to what will follow in the body of your paragraph.

_____

_____

_____

WRITING

Summary Paragraph

On a separate sheet of paper, write a summary of the news article on page 33. Begin with a topic sentence. Follow this with three sentences that support and explain the topic sentence. Avoid choppy sentences that waste words. Use your answers to "Getting Ready to Write" (pages 33–34) to help you.

SKILL BUILDING

Homophones

Homophones are words that sound alike but have different meanings and spellings. For example, the words *blue* and *blew* are homophones.

I.

In the story that follows, pairs of homophones are underlined. Circle the homophone in each pair that is correct for the sentence. You may use a dictionary if you need help. The first one has been done for you.

Medicine in the Olden Days

Imagine that you have a stomachache. You go to/too a doctor. To take care of your problem, the doctor hands you some small iron balls covered with butter and tells you to swallow them! Naturally, you don't get better, sew/so the doctor sends you to the hospital. When you get two/to the hospital, you find that it is a very dirty and bad-smelling place. The nurses put you in bed. But you

34

are not/knot alone. Their/There are four or five other people in the same bed with you!

Believe it oar/or not, it wasn't so very long ago that people received medical treatments like these. Medicine used to be/bee part superstition. Doctors often did not no/know what caused certain illnesses. Cures were largely a matter of luck and guesswork. Only within the last 100 years or so has the kind of medical care we enjoy today come into being.

Doctors in ancient times new/knew very little about how the body works. For example, the Greeks believed that people thought with they're/their hearts and that the brain's job was to control the heart. The ancient Greeks also believed that the heart maid/made blood instead of pumping it. Just 300 years ago, doctors still did not understand how nerves and muscles work. They thought that muscle movements were caused by/buy "explosions" of blood inside the body.

People often turned to their religious beliefs in hopes of finding a cure for disease. Sometimes they got carried away. For example, we know that during the Middle Ages ill people would/wood try to heel/heal themselves by licking the statues of saints.

All kinds of "cures" have been tried throughout the centuries. In ancient Egypt, for instance, taking the right medicine would sometimes mean swallowing dead mice. For skin problems, doctors in Babylonia told patients to take baths in beer. And we've/weave already mentioned buttered iron balls. They were prescribed for stomach trouble during colonial times in America. Doctors felt that it was best to take the buttered balls "on the full of the moon. A bit of lion's main/mane hung under the left arm," they added, "would also help."

Even today, of course/coarse, doctors dew/do not know everything about the human body. They have not yet one/won the last battle against disease. But today's doctors can usually give helpful treatment and sound advice. To be sure/shore, your/you're family doctor would give you something better to take than a handful of buttered iron balls!

Following are some homophones and their meanings. Study them before going on to the next activity.

their—belonging to them. Example: *Their* dog is old.
they're—contraction of "they are." Example: *They're* going to the store.
there—that something is, or where something is. Example: The book is over
    there.
not—form of *no.* Example: He is *not* at home.
knot—tie in a rope, thread, string, etc. Example: I couldn't tighten the *knot* in
    the rope.
wood—what trees are made of. Example: We built the table out of *wood.*
would—form of the verb *will.* Example: They said they *would* leave soon.

II.

Use each of the following words in an *original* sentence—one you make up yourself.

1. they're: _____

2. would: _____

3. not: _____

4. their: _____

5. knot: _____

6. there: _____

7. wood: _____

THINKING ABOUT WRITING

1. Does the summary you wrote begin with a topic sentence? If so, underline it. If not, write a topic sentence for it on your paper.

2. Are there any unnecessary sentences in your paragraph? If so, cross them out.

3. Have you used a series of choppy sentences that could be combined into one effective sentence? If so, rewrite them as a single sentence on your own paper.

SKILL BUILDING

4. Reread your summary. Did you use any homophones incorrectly? Correct any homophone errors you find.

5. Look for the following in your summary: incorrect end-of-sentence punctuation, capitalization errors, incorrect pronoun case. Correct any errors you find.

IT'S NEWS TO ME

News stories are often about major events, events that are important to many people. A news story may report someone going to space, the sinking of a ship, or the election of a president. Major news stories are either international or national—they are of interest to people all over the world or throughout a specific country. Other stories are of local interest.

The events that occur in the lives of most people are usually ordinary events: a dog gets lost or a new couch arrives. Stories of these events would not be printed in a newspaper. But they are important to the people involved and are worth sharing with friends and relatives.

Some junior and senior high school students were asked to become reporters. Their stories report everyday events from their lives.

MOWER BREAKS DOWN, THREATENS PARTY

By David Cando

Montgomery, Alabama—Mr. August Cando's power lawn mower broke down while he was mowing his back lawn at about three o'clock yesterday afternoon.

"I pulled on the starter, and the cord just pulled right out," stated Mr. Cando.

The Cando family was planning an outdoor party with friends that evening. The grass needed cutting, and they did not want their friends to see it that way.

Cando borrowed a mower from his next-door neighbor, Mrs. Martha Flores. He was able to get the lawn mowed in time for the party.

DOG OKAY AFTER TANGLING WITH CYCLE

By Ruth Switzer

Atlanta, Georgia—Tuffy, a dog belonging to Susan Avila, was struck by a motorcycle yesterday at 9:30 A.M. in front of the Avila's residence on Brook Street. The dog was chasing the motorcycle at the time.

Tuffy was taken to Westminster Dog and Cat Hospital. He was suffering from several cuts on his head and neck and a badly bruised right hind leg.

The veterinarian, Dr. Charles Gold, released Tuffy the same afternoon. Tuffy is reported in good condition, and he is resting comfortably at home.

According to an eyewitness, Tuffy ran barking after the vehicle. The dog was hit by the front wheel as the driver, Richard Yasuhiro, tried to turn a corner.

GIRAFFES BOW AGAIN IN 34-9 SOFTBALL DEFEAT

By Matthew Bernal

San Fernando, California—The Northridge Giraffes lost by the score of 34 to 9 to the Chatsworth Cruisers at Reseda Park last night in another embarrassing defeat.

The Cruisers scored 10 runs in the first inning and 6 in the third. Two grand slams in the fifth inning and 8 walks in the sixth accounted for most of the remaining runs scored by them.

The Giraffes scored all their runs in the seventh and final innings. In both innings, the Cruisers had let their first baseman, Ralph Snyder, take the mound and try his hand at pitching.

It was the sixth straight loss (in six games) for the Giraffes. The Cruisers are 4 and 2 on the season.

THINKING ABOUT WHAT YOU HAVE READ

Answer in complete sentences.

1. Why was getting the lawn cut important to August Cando?

_____

_____

_____

2. How would you have reacted if you were riding the motorcycle that struck Tuffy?

_____

_____

_____

3. The sports story by Matthew Bernal has some humorous aspects to it. What are some of the funny things reported in this story?

_____

_____

_____

4. Which of the three stories is most like one you might find in a local newspaper? Explain.

_____

_____

_____

5. Look carefully at the news story by David Cando. Which paragraph gives the most important details? Look at the other news stories. Which paragraph is the most important in each one? Write the first sentence of the most important paragraph in each story.

_____

_____

_____

_____

_____

THINKING ABOUT WRITING

Understanding Newspaper Writing

The opening sentences of a news story give the reader all the most important facts. They are called the _lead_. They tell the reader WHAT happened, WHEN it happened, WHERE it happened, and WHO was involved. Usually, they tell HOW and WHY it happened, too. These facts are called the _5 Ws_. Look back at the news story by Ruth Switzer, on page 38. Notice that all these important facts are given in the first paragraph. The 5 _Ws_ are listed below.

Tuffy, a dog belonging to Susan Avila,
      (who)

was struck by a motorcycle
      (what)

yesterday at 9:30 A.M.
      (when)

in front of the Avila's residence.
      (where)

The dog was chasing the motorcycle at the time.
      (why/how)

I.

Following are the first two sentences of a news story. Read them. Then, on the lines following the sentences, list the 5 *W*s.

Yesterday at 11 A.M., Robert Scotti and Doug Edwards sank while trying to row an old bathtub across Jinx Lake in Placer Valley, Oregon. Scotti accidentally knocked out the stopper and was unable to get it back in place before the heavy craft went under.

1. WHO:

    _____

    _____

2. WHAT:

    _____

    _____

3. WHERE:

    _____

    _____

4. WHEN:

    _____

    _____

5. WHY OR HOW:

    _____

    _____

6. Read the following 5 *W*s. Then, on a separate sheet of paper, use the facts to write the first two sentences of a news story.

WHO:	Randy Allen, a ninth grader at Penn High,
WHAT:	fell into a pig pen
WHERE:	his grandmother's ranch—ranch is in Ojai, California
WHEN:	yesterday—in the afternoon—about 4 P.M.
WHY OR HOW:	he was swinging from a tree, branch was over the pig pen, branch broke

At the top of a news story there is a *headline.* This is meant to catch the attention of the reader. The *byline* tells who wrote the story. It appears below the headline. The *dateline* tells where and sometimes when the story originated. It appears in the first line of the body of some news stories. The first one or two paragraphs are called the *lead.* The lead contains the 5 Ws.

EXAMPLE:

**BOY SMOLDERS
OVER
BURNED UP SOCKS**

Headline ⟨

Byline ▶ **By Joseph Wilder**

Dateline ▶ *Portland, Oregon*—A pair of tennis socks belonging to Carl Healy was burned up today when his younger brother, Michael Healy, age 3, put them in the oven to dry them. The socks had gotten soaked while Carl was hiking in woods near his home.

Lead ⟨

II.

Go back to the three news stories on pages 37 through 38. For each story, underline the *byline,* circle the *dateline,* and draw a box around the *lead.*

Getting Ready to Write

Soon you will be writing a news story. The following activity will help you get ready to write.

I.

1. Think of something that happened to you within the last few days. It can be something as ordinary as going to your friend's house for supper or as extraordinary as seeing a tornado or winning a contest. Briefly describe what happened.

   _____

   _____

   _____

   _____

2. Now think back to something that happened to you long ago. Briefly explain what happened.

_____

_____

_____

3. As homework, ask a friend or a relative to describe a personal experience that happened either recently or some time in the past. Describe what the person told you.

_____

_____

_____

II.

1. Think about your three answers above. Which one do you think would make the best news story? Explain.

_____

_____

2. Write a headline for the news-story idea you chose.

_____

3. Write a lead paragraph.

_____

_____

_____

_____

WRITING

News Story

On a separate sheet of paper, write a news story. Use your answers to "Getting Ready to Write" (pages 41 and 42) to help you. Be sure to include a headline, a byline, and a dateline. Remember to include the 5 Ws in the lead. Then add at least two more paragraphs.

SKILL BUILDING

Sentence Fragments

A sentence expresses a complete thought. A fragment does not express a complete thought. Most often, this is because a fragment lacks a subject, a verb, or both. Notice how the following fragment can be changed into a complete sentence by adding a subject and a verb.

(fragment): Two snakes near her hand.
(sentence): <u>Teri</u> <u>saw</u> two snakes near her hand.

A fragment can also result when the main verb needs a helping verb (or verbs).

(no helping verb): Mike gone for two years.

(helping verbs added): Mike <u>had</u> <u>been</u> gone for two years.

Some common helping verbs are:

am	has	can (may) have
are	had	could (would, should) be
is	can	could (would, should) have
was	may	will (shall) have been
were	will (shall) be	might have
do	will (shall) have	might have been
did	has (had) been	must
have	can (may) be	must have
		must have been

The following news story contains many fragments. Some need a subject, some need a verb, and others need a helping verb. Make each fragment a complete sentence by adding the necessary word or words. Insert the words between the lines. One word has been added for you.

TURTLE TURNS INTO A LIFEBOAT

By Drew Perry

Manila, Philippines—Three days ago a ship named the *Aloha* ^caught^ fire and sank 600 miles from land. Connie Villanueva, a pas-senger, was rescued by a huge turtle, which carried her to safety on shore.

Ms. Villanueva able to put on a life jacket and jump overboard before the *Aloha* disappeared beneath the waves. For

43

more than 12 hours she floated in the water. Suddenly a giant sea turtle appeared next to her. The next thing she knew, found herself riding across the ocean on the back of the turtle.

For the next day and a half carried Ms. Villanueva across the water. Finally she a boat in the distance.

The turtle turned in the direction of the boat. Swimming confidently, carried Ms. Villanueva to the craft.

A sailor standing on deck. Spotted the woman and threw her a life ring. Trembling from exhaustion and cold, Ms. Villanueva pulled aboard.

Before being taken to a cabin, Ms. Villanueva went to the railing. Looked down at the turtle that had saved her life. Strangely, the turtle looking up at her.

Then the turtle did something else unusual. Began swimming around the boat. "Circled the boat twice," said Ms. Villanueva. "Then looked back at me. It as if it wanted to make sure I was really okay. Then turned and disappeared into the water."

THINKING ABOUT WRITING

1. Take a second look at the news story you wrote. Does it contain a headline, a byline, and a dateline? If not, add these now.

2. Your lead paragraph should contain the 5 Ws. On the lines that follow, list the details in your lead paragraph that answer these questions.

   WHO? _____

   _____

   WHAT? _____

   _____

   WHERE? _____

   _____

   WHEN? _____

   _____

   WHY OR HOW? _____

   _____

   If some of these details are missing, rewrite your lead paragraph to include them.

3. Make sure your news story is broken into paragraphs. Also, make sure your paragraphs follow one another in a logical, easy-to-follow order. If you find any problems with the order of your paragraphs, rewrite the news story.

SKILL BUILDING

4. Check for sentence fragments in your news story. Correct any you find.

5. Write the first five words you capitalized in your news story. Be prepared to explain why each one is capitalized. You may use the capitalization rules on page 6 to help you.

6. Check your news story for errors in pronoun case, homophones, and end-of-sentence punctuation. Correct any errors you find.

PLAYFUL CONVERSATIONS

What would it be like if walls could talk? Or how about trees? Or rocks?

We asked some teenagers from Boston, Massachusetts, to write conversations with nonliving things. Here are some humorous and unusual plays they wrote.

In the Dark

(*I'm sitting in my room. I'm talking to the darkness in my closet.*)

ME: How's it going, Darkness?

D: Not too well. I'm depressed.

ME: Why?

D: Because I'm in this closet all the time. Why don't you let me out?

ME: You know I can't do that.

D: Why not?

ME: Because you're never there when I open the door.

D: What?

ME: As soon as I open the door, the light gets in and I can't see you.
D: You've got a point.
ME: You're the only thing in the world that's harder to see when there's light.
D: Well, why don't you come in and close the door. We could be together!
ME: No offense, but I don't like being alone with you.
(Darkness *sniffles*.)
ME: Now, don't cry! If you don't cry I'll come in and stay with you for a few minutes.
D: Thanks!
(*I go into the closet and shut the door.*)

Roger Mandretti

Talking to a Rock

(*I am sitting in the backyard. I'm talking to my favorite rock.*)
ME: Hi, Rocky.
ROCK:
ME: I said, "Hi, Rocky." Now, answer me.
ROCK:
ME: What's wrong? How come you aren't talking to me?
ROCK:
ME: This silent treatment won't work; I'm telling you. If you're sore about something, just tell me.
ROCK:
ME: I'm getting tired of your silly game. Now, say something! You're just playing games with me, aren't you?
ROCK:
ME: I'm really getting mad!
ROCK:
ME: I'm leaving!
ROCK:
ME: I've really had it with you!
ROCK: I'm sorry. I was just teasing. I won't do it any more.

Lynn Lofton

The Shirt on My Back

(*I'm sitting in my room. I'm talking to my shirt.*)
ME: Hi, Shirt.
S: Don't talk to me!
ME: Why not?
S: Because you got catsup on me at lunch. I'm tired of your carelessness.
ME: Sorry.
S: And another thing. . . .
ME: What's that?
S: Stop playing football. You get me all sweaty.
ME: I like playing football.
S: Well, I don't. I want you to quit.

ME: Never.
S: Do as you're told.
ME: Stop bossing me around.
S: You're a rotten kid, and it's about time you shaped up.
ME: You know what, Shirt?
S: What?
ME: I don't like you anymore. You nag too much.
S: Oh, really?
ME: Yes! Why don't you just get off my back!
(*I take off my shirt and throw it on the ground.*)

Dan O'Brian

THINKING ABOUT WHAT YOU HAVE READ

Answer in complete sentences.

1. How is the play "Talking to a Rock" different from the others? Explain.

_____

_____

_____

2. In which play does the nonliving thing have the nastiest disposition? Give reasons for your answer.

_____

_____

_____

3. What sort of personality does Darkness have in the play "In the Dark"? Discuss.

_____

_____

_____

4. A play contains dialogue (talk between people) and narration (description of action). Read the narration at the beginning of each play. How are the opening narrations similar?

_____

_____

_____

THINKING ABOUT WRITING

Figurative Language

Without thinking about it, you have probably used *figures of speech* such as the following: *She runs like lightning. The town was gripped by fear. Life is a long, hard road.*

A **figure of speech**—or **figurative language**—is a comparison of one thing with something that it really is not. For example, life is not actually a road. But the figure of speech *life is a long, hard road* conveys a thought or a feeling about life in a colorful and unusual way. Also, it compares life to something that has (or that suggests) a meaning familiar to many people: a long, hard road.

Writers use many types of figures of speech. In this lesson, you will be introduced to three of these. They are the *simile*, the *metaphor*, and the *personification*.

A **simile** is a comparison in which the word *like* or *as* is used.

> **EXAMPLES:** I slept <u>like</u> a log last night.
> He can throw a football <u>as</u> straight <u>as</u> an arrow.

I.

Complete each of the following similes on the lines provided. Use as many words as are needed.

1. The stars were spread across the sky like _____

    _____

2. His hair looked like _____

    _____

3. His voice sounded far away, as if it were coming from _____

    _____

4. The four of them stood there like _____

    _____

5. (Write an original simile.) _____

    _____

A **metaphor** is a comparison in which the word *like* or *as* is NOT used. For example, "Love is a battlefield" is a metaphor, a comparison of one thing with another without using *like* or *as*.

II.

Change each of the following similes into metaphors by crossing out key words.

> **EXAMPLE:** Her eyes were ~~like~~ two shiny stars.

1. The desert was like an oven.

2. The river is as dirty as a sewer.

3. The night is like a friend to me.

4. Life is like a corridor, down which we walk toward the darkness.

5. It was as if the world were a playground.

6. Love is sometimes like a flower that blooms but never dies.

7. Love is like a light that brightens every person on which it shines.

8. (Write an original metaphor.)

_____

_____

_____

_____

_____

Personification is another type of figurative language. It gives human or animal characteristics to nonhuman things—things like leaves and mountains and raindrops. For example, the sentence, "The tall palm trees danced in the wind, their grass skirts swirling and swishing," is a personification. Using only words, we have made the palm trees into hula dancers.

III.

Read the following personifications. Then on the lines, name the type of person the nonhuman thing is being compared to.

> **EXAMPLE:** The sea wrote poems upon the sand, using words known only to itself.
>
> The sea is described as if it were a _____*poet*_____.

1. The swirling wind shuffled the leaves and then dealt them all again.

   The wind is described as if it were a _____.

2. The mountain sat upon his throne and viewed the splendid realm.

   The mountain is described as if it were a _____.

3. The soaking rain gave the earth an injection of life-giving serum.

   The rain is described as if it were a _____.

4. That night, Death sneaked into our house and stole our child away.

   Death is described as if it were a _____.

5. Autumn comes with invisible scissors to shave and trim the trees' old heads.

   Autumn is described as if it were a _____.

IV.

Each underlined statement in the following play is either a *simile,* a *metaphor,* or a *personification.* In the blank beside each of these lines, write either *simile, metaphor,* or *personification.* The first answer is given as an example. You may look back at the examples in activities I, II, and III to help you.

Getting to the Point

(*Mickey Mouth is returning from a date with Judy DeCutie. They stand on the front step of Judy's home, saying goodnight.*)

MICKEY: Your hair is like golden thread.   *simile*

JUDY: What?

MICKEY: And your eyes are two sparkling diamonds.   1. _____

JUDY: Oh, thanks.

MICKEY: Indeed, your whole lovely face is a mirror reflecting my

love.   2. _____

JUDY: It is?

MICKEY: (*taking her hand*): And your tiny hand is but a flower in my

palm.   3. _____

JUDY: Really!

MICKEY: (*points upward at the sky*): Oh, and look up at the night.

Sweet Mr. Night is smiling down on us.   4. _____

JUDY: He is?

MICKEY: And the stars—they dance across the universe on silver-tipped feet.

5. _____

JUDY: What?

MICKEY: (*puts an arm around her*): Oh, Judy, this evening with you has been like a dream.

6. _____

JUDY: Glad you liked it.

MICKEY: Oh, indeed I did. It was like a few hours adrift in heaven.

7. _____

JUDY: It was?

MICKEY: Oh, yes, dear Judy. And it shall never end, for Mr. Future is opening his arms to us, telling us to go forward with our love.

8. _____

JUDY: How weird!

MICKEY: And may I say that another date with you would be like taking an elevator to eternal happiness.

9. _____

JUDY: Are you trying to say you want to go out with me again?

MICKEY: Yes. How about Friday?

JUDY: Sure, but why didn't you just say so? You've been standing here talking like a crazy person for ten minutes.

10. _____

MICKEY: Guess I did get a little carried away.

JUDY: Yes, a little.

Getting Ready to Write

Soon you will write a play that consists of a conversation between you and an object.

I.

Below, circle the one object you would like to use in your play. If none of these appeals to you, write your own idea in the blank.

tree   grain of sand   football   star   book   chair   shoe   house   stocking

steps   roll of tape   TV   pen   lake   mountain   car   stove   record player

candle   ocean   fan   carpet   doll   couch   scissors   the wind   flower

coloring book   flag   _____

II.

Complete the following sentences. This will form the opening narration of your play.

I am sitting in my _____. I am talking with _____.

III.

How would you begin a conversation with the object you chose in Part I above? Write some ideas of opening lines of dialogue.

_____

_____

IV.

How might you end your play? Write some of your ideas.

_____

Short Play

On a separate sheet of paper, write a short play that consists of a conversation between you and an object. Use your answers to "Getting Ready to Write" (above) to help you. Use the plays on pages 46 through 48 as models.

SKILL BUILDING

Subject-Verb Agreement

A singular subject names one thing. For example, all of the following are singular:

    she   Mr. Stringbean   the rattlesnake

A singular subject takes a singular verb. Singular verbs in the present tense end in *s* or *es*. For example:

    she watch*es*   Mr. Stringbean yell*s*   the rattlesnake coil*s*

A plural subject needs a plural verb. Plural verbs in the present tense do not end in *s* or *es*.

    she and I watch   Mr. and Mrs. Stringbean yell   the rattlesnakes coil

I.

Complete each item that follows by inserting a singular subject in the blank.

EXAMPLE: _____That_____ seems like a good idea.

1. _____ looks bad for us.

2. _____ usually thinks of something.

3. In the morning, _____ gargles with Bubble-Gulp mouthwash.

4. During those tests, _____ starts to ache.

5. Furthermore, _____ needs a bath.

The verb *be* is the verb used most often, and it is *irregular*. That is, it does not follow regular rules for changing from the singular to the plural or from the present to the past tense. Study the following chart for the verb *be*.

PRESENT TENSE		PAST TENSE	
I am	we are	I was	we were
you are	you are	you were	you were
he, she, or it is	they are	he, she, or it was	they were
(Joan *or* Mike <u>is</u>)	(Joan *and* Mike <u>are</u>)	(Joan *or* Mike <u>was</u>)	(Joan *and* Mike <u>were</u>)

II.

Complete each of the following items by inserting the correct *present tense* form of the verb *be*. Write *am, are,* or *is* in the blanks.

    EXAMPLE: He _____*is*_____ here now.

1. They _____ leaving for school.

2. I _____ right here.

3. The dog _____ barking.

4. Ralph or Mike _____ coming back.

III.

Complete each of the following items by inserting the correct *past tense* form of the verb *be*.

    EXAMPLE: You _____*were*_____ talking too much.

1. I _____ there yesterday.

2. This morning they _____ sleepy.

3. A couple days ago it _____ in the cupboard.

4. Yesterday Bob or Janet _____ there to help.

Making the verb agree with the subject is not easy if you cannot find the subject. Finding the subject is especially hard in a sentence such as this:

    One of the boys sells newspapers.

    The subject of this sentence is *one.* The word *boys* is the object of the preposition *of.* The verb *sells* agrees with the subject, *one,* and is singular.

IV.

In each of the following sentences, underline the subject and circle the correct verb.

1. A dog with fleas are/is in the yard.

2. The cats in the tree looks/look scared.

3. The woman wearing the bracelets seem/seems nice.

4. The samples of wallpaper is/are pretty.

5. The box of staples is/are on the desk.

THINKING ABOUT WRITING

1. The play you wrote has the overall effect of creating a long personification. That is, you gave human or animal characteristics to something that is not alive. What object did you personify? What sort of personality did you give this thing? (For example, was it cheerful? Was it grumpy?) Explain below.

_____

_____

_____

2. Did you use any figures of speech in the dialogue of your play? Are there any one-line similes, metaphors, or personifications? If so, underline them.

3. Did you give a title to your play? If not, do so now.

4. Ask a classmate to read your play. Ask your classmate whether the dialogue sounds logical and natural. Make any changes that might improve your play.

SKILL BUILDING

5. Reread your play. Are there any instances in which a subject and a verb do not agree? Make whatever corrections are necessary.

6. Are there any fragments in your play? If so, rewrite them on your paper as complete sentences.

7. Look for all the following in your play: capitalization errors, incorrect pronoun case, incorrect end-of-sentence punctuation, homophone errors. Correct any errors you find.

FRIENDLY PERSUASION

Imagine you have a 25-year-old cousin named Archie. You like Archie, but he is a pretty unusual character. For example, two years ago, on a whim, Archie spent all his savings on an old, leaky houseboat. Then he tried to sail down the Mississippi River. The houseboat sank, and Cousin Archie barely escaped.

Now Archie has another wild scheme. He has just written a letter informing you that he is flying to the People's Republic of Desertia. There he plans to open a store, selling boats and marine equipment. Desertia is a country with no coastline. There is a huge tax on anything related to water sports. Besides, no one can swim.

How can you persuade Archie not to go through with his silly plan? What could you say in a letter to him to dissuade him? This is the question we asked students in Chicago, Illinois. We asked them to write letters persuading Archie to change his mind. A few of these letters follow.

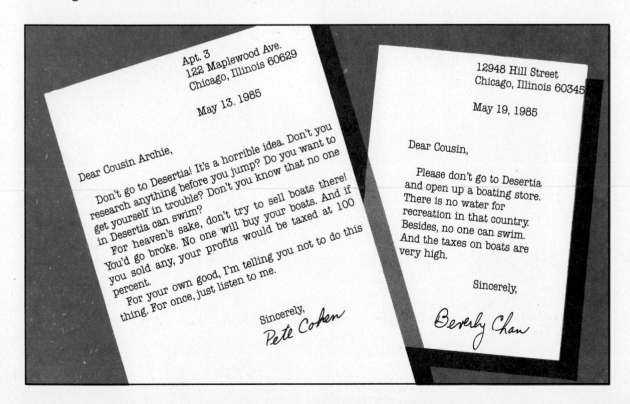

Apt. 3
122 Maplewood Ave.
Chicago, Illinois 60629

May 13, 1985

Dear Cousin Archie,

Don't go to Desertia! It's a horrible idea. Don't you research anything before you jump? Do you want to get yourself in trouble? Don't you know that no one in Desertia can swim?

For heaven's sake, don't try to sell boats there! You'd go broke. No one will buy your boats. And if you sold any, your profits would be taxed at 100 percent.

For your own good, I'm telling you not to do this thing. For once, just listen to me.

Sincerely,
Pete Cohen

12948 Hill Street
Chicago, Illinois 60345

May 19, 1985

Dear Cousin,

Please don't go to Desertia and open up a boating store. There is no water for recreation in that country. Besides, no one can swim. And the taxes on boats are very high.

Sincerely,
Beverly Chan

1992 Vincennes Ave., S.
Chicago, Illinois 60615

May 14, 1985

Dear Archie,

I have just read your letter about going to Desertia to open a marine supply and boat store. I have to say I respect your spirit of adventure. Still, I think there are a lot of reasons you shouldn't do this.

Remember what happened when you bought that houseboat two years ago? It was a great idea in some ways, but it really didn't work out well at all. If you had thought about it beforehand, I don't think you would have done it.

Also, there are some things about Desertia you may not know. No one in Desertia can swim. The taxes there are very high on boats and marine equipment. Apparently, the government wants to discourage water sports. You won't make any money from your store.

Flying is a very popular sport in Desertia. Almost half the adult population has a pilot's license. You might give some thought to selling parachutes and flying suits instead.

Of course, it's your decision. I hope you don't mind my expressing an opinion. I just thought it was important to let you know how I feel.

Your cousin,
Carol Stram

127 Winchester Ave., N., Apt. 14
Chicago, Illinois 60622

May 23, 1985

Dear Cousin Archie,

I had to laugh when I read your goofy letter about going to Desertia. You shouldn't do it. Take my word for it, this is a ridiculous thing to do. Please don't do it. You would be foolish. The Desertians can't even swim. Please don't do it. It's a silly idea.

Sincerely,
Bob Riles

THINKING ABOUT WHAT YOU HAVE READ

Answer in complete sentences.

1. Which letter most comes across as though the writer is giving orders? Explain.

   _____

   _____

2. Which of the letters has redundancies? That is, in which one does the writer repeat herself or himself? Cite examples of redundancy from the letter.

   _____

   _____

   _____

3. The word *tactful* means saying or doing something in a way that won't offend. In her letter, Carol Stram says several tactful things. For example, she says: "I hope you don't mind my expressing an opinion." What other tactful phrases and sentences can you find in her letter? Write them below.

   _____

   _____

   _____

   _____

4. Carol Stram's letter contains specific details to persuade Archie not to go to Desertia. What are some of the facts she points out? What suggestion does she offer as an alternative?

   _____

   _____

   _____

5. Beverly Chan uses the same details. But does she do so as effectively as Carol Stram? Explain your answer.

   _____

   _____

6. Which of the letters, in your opinion, is best? Explain your answer.

   _____

   _____

THINKING ABOUT WRITING

Format, Facts, and Tact

In writing a friendly letter, you should use the form shown below.

747 Airplane Ave.
Runway, Ohio 70701 } **Heading**

October 31, 1990

Salutation ▶ Dear Mr. Fluzz,

Did you know that the body of a letter is what you actually have to say? It's all the things you write to the other person, after the *salutation*.

Well, that's all I wanted to teach you for now. Maybe the next time I write I'll teach you something else. } **Body**

Closing ▶ Sincerely yours,

Signature ▶ *Freddie*

P.S. Sometimes a letter has a postscript. Write a P.S. when you have forgotten to say something in the body of a letter. } **Postscript**

I.

All of the parts (including the paragraphs in the body) of the letter on page 61 are in the wrong place. Study the letter carefully, comparing it with the proper form, as shown above. Rewrite it on a separate sheet of paper, putting all the parts where they should be.

Do they have letter-writing classes where you live, too? If so, you really should take one. Then you'd be able to write great letters, just like mine!

Sincerely yours,

Joe Letterman

P.S.

Mom just asked me to ask you if you got the 300-pound bag of duck food we sent you. Please let us know.

I'm taking a class in letter writing, and I'm really enjoying it. You can see by this letter how much I've learned.

999 Rancho Street

November 33, 1989

Cowboyville, California

Dear Mrs. Worsworth,

Well, that's all for now. Write back soon.

Sometimes when you write a letter, your goal is to persuade someone to do something for you. For example, you may want to persuade someone to loan you money to buy a bicycle.

If you want to be successful in getting the loan, you should give the person you are writing to some specific reasons for helping you. Just saying you want the money is usually not enough. The person might be more willing to help if you were to give the following specific facts: You need just $50 more to buy a ten-speed bicycle; if you have the bike, you are sure you can get a job working for a messenger service; within two weeks after getting the job, you will be able to pay back the money.

II.

Imagine you are writing to your cousins Linda and Doug. You want to persuade them to come and visit you for two weeks during the summer. On a separate sheet of paper, make a list of some of the things you could say to get them to visit.

EXAMPLE:
The beach is close, and we could go as often as you like.

The word *tactful,* as you know, means saying or writing something in a way that won't offend. It means putting things in a polite and considerate way.

III.

The sentences in each pair below say nearly the same thing. One is tactful,
while the other is not. Circle the letter next to the tactful sentence.

1. **a.** I guess you had as much trouble with math last semester as I had with social studies.
    b. I heard you got a fat *D* in math last semester.

2. **a.** None of the kids I introduced you to liked you at all.
    b. You and those kids didn't get along. That happens sometimes.

3. **a.** I hope you don't mind my saying that eating junk food can cause skin problems.
    b. You're going to have bad skin if you keep eating junk food.

4. **a.** May I bring some of my records to your next party?
    b. Why don't you play some decent records at your next party?

Getting Ready to Write

Remember Cousin Archie? Archie has a new harebrained scheme. He's going
to ride his moped up the 10,000-foot Mount Oudumiu!

You are going to be writing a letter addressed to Archie. The purpose of
your letter will be to persuade him tactfully that he should not go through with
his plan. The following will help you get ready to write.

Below are some reasons why Archie shouldn't try to drive his moped up
Mount Oudumiu. You may use any or all of these facts in your letter.

1. There has been an outbreak of Gungy fever in the Oudumiu area.

2. Archie's moped can barely make it up a slight grade on a paved road. The slopes of Oudumiu
    are ice-covered and almost vertical.

3. It would cost over $30,000 for the expedition.

Letter of Persuasion

On a separate sheet of paper, write a letter to Archie. Persuade him not to
attempt the trip up Mount Oudumiu on his moped. Give him good reasons for
canceling the trip. Be tactful.

Use the correct format for a friendly letter. Use the information in "Getting
Ready to Write" (above) to help you.

SKILL BUILDING

Avoiding Run-Ons

A **run-on sentence** is one that keeps going on and on and on. Usually, it consists of two or more separate, complete thoughts that have been joined, using conjunctions such as *and, or, so, but, because,* and *then.*

Study the run-on below. Notice how it can be repaired by putting a period at the end of the first sentence and crossing out the word *and.*

(run-on): At one time, stamps and envelopes were not separate items and the stamp was printed directly on the envelope.

(correct): At one time, stamps and envelopes were not separate items. ~~and~~ The stamp was printed directly on the envelope.

Repair the run-ons in the following selection. Put a period at the end of each sentence. Cross out each unnecessary *and, or, so, but, because,* or *then.* Capitalize the first word of the next sentence. The first change has been made for you.

The Unopened Letter

One day in 1848 a letter arrived for General Zachary Taylor at his home in Baton Rouge, Louisiana ~~and~~ As was common in those days, the letter had no stamp on it then also, the letter was marked *collect,* which meant that the person receiving the letter had to pay for delivery and this greatly annoyed Taylor then he refused delivery and had the unopened letter returned to its sender

Taylor did not know it at the time, but the letter he had sent back was probably the most

important one he would receive in his life and the letter, as it turned out, informed him that he had been nominated for the presidency of the United States

Taylor eventually got the news of his nomination so a year later, in 1849, he was elected the 12th president of the United States

The story of General Taylor's unopened letter helps to show how inadequate the postal service was at that time because the fee for handling letters was sometimes paid by the sender, sometimes by the receiver and some letters had stamps on them and others had handwritten symbols, and others had no postal markings at all

Our postal system today is not perfect but to be sure, however, it is a great deal better than it was in General Taylor's day

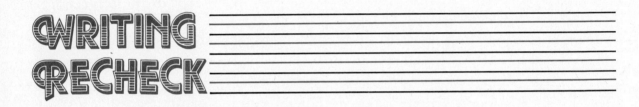

THINKING ABOUT WRITING

1. Compare the format of the letter you wrote with that shown on page 60. Make any necessary corrections.

2. Underline those sentences or phrases in your letter that you feel are tactful.

3. Below, list the facts you used to persuade Archie not to go ahead with his plan.

_____

_____

_____

_____

4. Does your letter have a postscript (P.S.)? If not, add one.

SKILL BUILDING

5. Look for all of the following in your letter: run-ons, fragments, incorrect end-of-sentence punctuation, errors in subject-verb agreement, incorrect use of homophones, incorrect pronoun case, capitalization errors. Correct any errors you find.

CWHAT'S THE POINT?

A story usually has a *theme*. A **theme** is an idea or a message that a reader gets from a story. It is the point that the author makes, through the story, about life.

Try to find the theme of the following story.

Beautiful, Curly Hair

Thurgood Thistlewizard was like any other 16-year-old, except that he had an unusual hobby. His hobby was inventing things in his home laboratory. Among other things, Thurgood had invented a pair of electric roller skates, a fertilizer that grew giant vegetables, and a mechanical dog named Tin Rin Rin.

Thurgood's latest idea concerned his hair. He had very curly hair, which he hated and which he wished were straight. He had tried every brand of straightener, but they only worked for a while. What Thurgood wanted was something that would straighten his hair for life.

After experimenting for several weeks, he finally mixed a lotion he was sure would do the trick. It was a combination of hydrofluffocene and extract of lizard tears. He called his sister Margie into his room and told her what he was going to do. Margie didn't like his idea, but Thurgood went ahead and rubbed the strange lotion into his hair. Then he sat back and waited.

All of a sudden his hair began to uncurl. But something else started happening too. Thurgood's hair began to grow rapidly. It was growing at the rate of several inches a second. His hair reached the floor, and then it started moving across the carpet. When it reached a table leg, it started to coil around it. Margie ran from the room.

Mr. and Mrs. Thistlewizard came running into Thurgood's room with scissors. They stared in shock as Margie and Thurgood tried to explain what had happened. Mrs. Thistlewizard started cutting the hair, but it kept growing. Margie stuffed the cut hair in bags and her father hauled it out of the house. They were frantic. No one knew what to do. No one, except Thurgood.

While his parents and sister worked, Thurgood worked out a formula for a new lotion—one to make his hair stop growing. Then he went to his workbench and poured a drop of H27R into a pint of tincture of fuzzball.

Thurgood's parents were afraid of what the new lotion might do, but it seemed like the only hope. Thurgood told them not to worry; then he poured the mixture on his scalp. Everybody watched to see what would happen.

All of a sudden Thurgood's hair stopped growing! His family started to applaud. But their joy didn't last long; not only had Thurgood's hair stopped growing longer, it had also started getting shorter! There was nothing his family could do. They just watched as Thurgood's hair got shorter and shorter, until he was completely bald!

Completely bald, Thurgood cried himself to sleep that night. "What have I done to myself?" he moaned. "What have I done?"

The next day there was only one thought in Thurgood's head: he would have to invent something that would make his hair grow again. He worked all day and all night. He tried bubble creams and sun treatments. He tried one thing after another, but nothing worked.

The days turned into weeks, and the weeks into months. Finally, Thurgood gave up. He could think of nothing more to do to get his hair back.

One morning he got out of bed, sad and unhappy as usual—until he looked in the mirror. Then his eyes lit up with joy. His head was covered with a bit of curly fuzz.

Gradually, nature gave Thurgood what he couldn't give himself. Each day the fuzz grew a little more. And soon his hair was back to normal.

Today, Thurgood is a very happy person. He has his hair back. Of course, it is very curly, just as it used to be. But Thurgood doesn't mind a bit. To him, it is the most beautiful hair in the world.

THINKING ABOUT WHAT YOU HAVE READ

Answer in complete sentences.

1. What happens because Thurgood tries to change his hair? Briefly summarize all that happens in the story.

   _____

   _____

   _____

   _____

   _____

2. Could it be that the theme of this story is, you should accept yourself the way you are? Explain.

   _____

   _____

   _____

   _____

   _____

3. In the beginning of the story, Thurgood dislikes his curly hair. Would the story have the same theme if it had been written about someone who disliked his or her *straight* hair? Explain.

   _____

   _____

   _____

   _____

4. At the end of the story, Thurgood has curly hair again. He thinks it is "the most beautiful hair in the world." Why have his feelings changed?

   _____

   _____

   _____

   _____

THINKING ABOUT WRITING

Themes

As you know, the theme of a piece of writing is the main idea or message behind it. It is the point about life the author is trying to get across to the reader. For example, imagine a story about a man who builds a machine that can tell people's future. In trying it out on himself, he learns of every bad thing that is going to happen to him. He gets terribly upset and depressed. He destroys the machine, wishing he had never built it—wishing he had never known about the future. The theme of that story would be: There are some things people are better off not knowing.

Study the following picture stories, then read the list of themes on page 69. Write the number of the appropriate picture story beside the letter of the correct theme. There are more themes given than you need.

THEMES

_____ **A.** Money isn't everything.

_____ **B.** You do not always save money by doing things yourself.

_____ **C.** Find time to be with your children—they won't be young forever.

_____ **D.** Nobody likes a braggart.

_____ **E.** Children don't think of their parents' feelings often enough.

_____ **F.** The easiest way to get a compliment is to give one.

_____ **G.** Don't say things unless you mean them.

_____ **H.** A bad boss is a terrible thing to have.

_____ **I.** Athletes should be nice to each other.

_____ **J.** Sometimes we take out our anger on the wrong people or things.

_____ **K.** It is better to give than to receive.

Getting Ready to Write

Soon you will be turning one of the picture stories on page 68 or 69 into a written story. The following activity will help you get ready to write. Write your answers on a separate sheet of paper.

1. Examine all the picture stories on pages 68 through 69. Choose the one you think would make the best and most interesting story. If you prefer, think of a story of your own—one that makes a point—and briefly describe it.

2. Write the names of all the characters in your story. (For example, the boss—Mr. Drillsergeant.)

3. Write a rough draft of the first three sentences of your story.

Story with a Theme

On a separate sheet of paper, write a story based on your own idea or on one of the picture stories shown on pages 68 through 69. Use your answers to "Getting Ready to Write" (above) to help you.

SKILL BUILDING

Punctuation

You have already learned about end-of-sentence punctuation marks. In the exercise that follows, you will learn about the punctuation marks shown above. The activity that follows is an introduction. It will help you get acquainted with the marks and how they are used.

Notice that the word *parentheSES* is plural; *parentheSIS* is singular. The first, or opening, parenthesis looks like this: **(**. The second, or closing, parenthesis, looks like this: **)**.

The following reading selection has *punctuation words* where *punctuation marks* should go. On a separate sheet of paper, rewrite the selection, changing the *punctuation words* into the *punctuation marks*.

EXAMPLE: Robert Louis Stevenson PARENTHESIS 1850 DASH 1894 PARENTHESIS thought of the plot of *Dr. Jekyll and Mr. Hyde* in a dream PERIOD

Robert Louis Stevenson **(**1850–1894**)** thought of the plot of *Dr. Jekyll and Mr. Hyde* in a dream**.**

Dickens's Strange Dream

Have you heard of Charles Dickens QUESTION MARK Dickens PARENTHESIS 1812 DASH 1870 PARENTHESIS is a famous English writer PERIOD He wrote the following novels COLON *Oliver Twist* COMMA *Pickwick Papers* COMMA *A Christmas Carol* COMMA *A Tale of Two Cities* COMMA and *Great Expectations* PERIOD

One night Dickens dreamed he saw a lady in a red shawl with her back to him PERIOD She turned around and said COMMA QUOTATION MARKS I am Miss Napier PERIOD QUOTATION MARKS Dickens didn APOSTROPHE t recognize the face SEMICOLON the name COMMA too COMMA was not that of anyone he knew PERIOD

The next day Dickens kept thinking about the dream PERIOD That evening he went out to a friend APOSTROPHE s house. And there was the lady DASH the lady in the red shawl EXCLAMATION POINT QUOTATION MARKS Good evening COMMA QUOTATION MARKS she said COMMA QUOTATION MARKS I am Miss Napier PERIOD QUOTATION MARKS

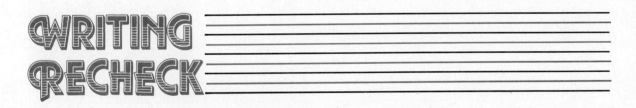

THINKING ABOUT WRITING

1. Ask at least two friends or relatives to read the story you wrote. Ask them whether they see the point you are trying to make with it. If neither sees the point, you should rewrite your story to make the theme more obvious.

2. Look carefully at the choice of words in your story. Are there any words you can replace with more effective ones? Make any changes you feel will improve your work.

SKILL BUILDING

3. Check your story for errors in any of the following areas: capitalization, end-of-sentence punctuation, pronoun case, homophones, fragments, subject-verb agreement, run-ons. Correct any errors you find.

COMIC RELIEF

The first known cartoon of several frames like the comic strips we enjoy today was printed in England in 1890. The cartoon was created by Alfred Harmsworth. It was called "Confessions of a Leave Man."

Seventeen-year-old Robert Guillen of Pacoima, California, continues the comic tradition. Below is one of his ideas.

THINKING ABOUT WHAT YOU HAVE READ

Answer in complete sentences.

1. What are the girl's reasons for not doing her homework?

   _____

   _____

   _____

2. In your opinion, had she been thinking beforehand about what she would say to her teacher? Explain.

   _____

   _____

   _____

3. How do you think the student feels when she finds out there wasn't any homework?

   _____

   _____

   _____

4. Have you ever been embarrassed in class or seen someone else embarrassed? Briefly describe what happened.

   _____

   _____

   _____

   _____

5. What do you think of the cartoon by Robert Guillen? Explain.

   _____

   _____

   _____

   _____

THINKING ABOUT WRITING

Cause and Effect

We see an almost endless variety of *cause-and-effect* relationships all the time. For example, imagine a dog chasing a cat. The dog knocks down a little boy. The boy falls against a ladder, knocking it to the ground. The boy's mother, who was up on the roof, now has no way to get down.

A **cause** is a reason for something happening. An **effect** is what happens as a result of the cause. For example, the boy's fall against the ladder (cause) knocks the ladder down (effect).

Carefully study the following "Peanuts" cartoon. Look for cause-and-effect relationships.

I.

The following cause-and-effect statements are about the "Peanuts" cartoon.
Only the cause is given. Complete each sentence by writing the effect. The
first one has been done for you.

1. Because Lucy puts Linus's security blanket in the dryer, he *cannot find it.*

2. Because Linus doesn't know where his security blanket is, he _____

   _____

3. Lucy throws the hot blanket to Linus. As a result, he _____

   _____

4. Because the blanket remains very hot, Linus _____

   _____

5. Because Linus cannot hold on to the blanket, Snoopy _____

   _____

6. The blanket is still hot. As a result, Snoopy _____

   _____

II.

Each of the following cartoons shows an effect. Use your imagination and
think of a possible cause for each effect. Write the cause for each cartoon on
a separate sheet of paper. Number your answers.

Getting Ready to Write

Soon you will create an original cartoon. That may sound difficult, but it's not. You do not even have to be able to draw well. All that is needed is a little planning.

I.

Look at the following cartoon pictures. Put a check (✔) beside the one you think you could draw and about which you could make up a simple story. If you prefer, do your own drawing in the empty frame.

II.

Think of a very short story based on the cartoon frame you chose in Part I. (You may use the words in the example frame to get yourself going.) For example, suppose you are going to create a cartoon about "The Rock and the Flower." The rock's wish to be a flower may be the main idea of your cartoon story.

Before you draw your cartoon, write what is going to happen in it. On the following lines, briefly describe what will happen in each frame. Be sure that cause-and-effect relationships are clear.

EXAMPLE: FRAME ONE

> *The rock is talking.*
> *It says it wants*
> *to be a flower.*

FRAME ONE	FRAME TWO	FRAME THREE	FRAME FOUR

Your Cartoon

Now, on a separate sheet of paper, create your own cartoon. Use the descriptions you wrote in Part II (above) to guide you.

SKILL BUILDING

The Comma

Study these rules of comma usage before doing the activities that follow.

Use the comma . . .

1. to set off explanatory words and phrases (apposition).
   Mr. Winston, my teacher, uses suspenders to hold up his pants.

2. to set off words and phrases such as *furthermore, therefore, also,* and *to begin with.*
   Furthermore, your socks are on backwards.
   You should not, however, keep your swim fins in the refrigerator.

3. to separate words, phrases, and clauses in a series.
   He ate the carrot, smiled at me, and turned orange.

4. between coordinate adjectives modifying the same noun. (If the word *and* can be placed between the adjectives, they are *coordinate.*)
   He had a weird, horrifying dream. (He had a weird AND horrifying dream.)
   NOTE: Do *not* separate noncoordinate adjectives (where *and* between the adjectives would sound strange).
   He was wearing pink rubber boots.

5. before coordinating conjunctions (*and, but, or, not, for, yet, so*) joining two independent clauses.
   He walked into class on his hands, but nobody noticed.

6. to set off the name of a person being spoken to.
   Mary, will you please come out of your room?

7. to set off introductory clauses or long phrases.
   Listening to him tell the story, we all had a good laugh.

8. to set off direct quotations.
   He looked at me and asked, "May I borrow your toothbrush?"

9. to set off a subordinate clause that comes before the main clause.
   Unless you promise not to bring your deadly spiders, you cannot come to my party.

10. to set off a subordinate clause that follows the main clause if the subordinate clause is not essential to the meaning of the sentence.
    You should all stay home, if only to make the party a success.
    NOTE: Do *not* set off essential clauses.
    I'll just die if he's there.

11. to enclose inserted sentence elements.
    I did it, not because I wanted to, but because I didn't know what I was doing.

The words and the punctuation marks in each sentence are scrambled. Un-scramble the sentences by putting both the words and the punctuation marks where they belong.

The comma rule next to each jumble will help you figure out the word order of the sentences and where the punctuation goes.

EXAMPLE: *(Rule 6)*   get you me that David ? for , will

David, will you get that for me?

1. *(Rule 2)*   did   do   ,   not   chores   .   Furthermore   your   you

   _____

2. *(Rule 6)*   quit   will   dog   .   Carol   you   that   ,   teasing

   _____

3. *(Rule 3)*   light   horseshoe   We   a   sweater   found   .   bulb   a   ,   a   ,   and   a

   _____

4. *(Rule 9)*   stay   to   goes   If   .   party   ,   I   home   he   the

   _____

5. *(Rule 7)*   needle   Seeing   suddenly   I   .   fainted   ,   the

   _____

6. *(Rule 1)*   was   ,   Mr.   the   sandwich   .   eating   ,   a   painter   Washington

   _____

7. *(Rule 4)*   wore   ,   She   grease-stained   dress   .   a   ,   long   purple

   _____

8. *(Rule 5)*   but   ,   It   getting   .   jacket   on   he   his   wouldn't   was   put   cold

   _____

9. *(Rule 11)*   it   Joe   did   .   Mike   ,   not   ,

   _____

10. *(Rule 3)*   the   stepped   ,   He   closet   shut   and   door   room   the   across   ,   the   walked   .   into

   _____

   _____

THINKING ABOUT WRITING

1. Study your cartoon. What cause-and-effect relationships do you see? Describe them on a separate sheet of paper.

2. What kinds of conflict occur in your cartoon? Describe them on your paper.

3. Are any sentences in your cartoon written in a confusing way? If so, rewrite each the way it should be.

4. Are there any figures of speech—similes, metaphors, or personifications—in your cartoon? List all that you find.

SKILL BUILDING

5. Study the rules of comma usage on page 78. Then reread your cartoon. Add necessary commas; get rid of those that do not belong.

6. A fragment is an incomplete thought. It lacks either a subject, a verb, or both. In most kinds of writing, fragments are not acceptable. However, this rule does not hold for cartoon writing. In cartoons, fragments are both common and generally acceptable. This is because cartoonists want their characters to speak as people do in everyday life. Everyday speech is filled with fragments.

   Look through your cartoon. See how many sentence fragments you can find. Write each on your paper. Next, rewrite each as a complete sentence.

   EXAMPLE:

7. Check for the following in your cartoon: capitalization errors, problems with subject-verb agreement, homophone errors, incorrect or missing end-of-sentence punctuation. Correct any errors you find.

PARTNER STORIES

Our memories are filled with true stories. When we get together with friends, we like to swap stories. We like to tell about some of the interesting things that have happened to us.

Illustrated below are two friends. Each is telling a story. Decide for yourself which of the two stories makes the most sense.

It hit me right in the head, and right into the hospital I went. The guy was Ronnie Morris, my best friend. The kids missed what happened who came later. It felt as if my head exploded! Ronnie had thrown a ball up in the air I didn't know. He took a swing at it and missed it and hit me on the noggin. We were waiting around for the other kids to show up for the baseball game. He threw the ball up in the air a few years ago and I caught it right on the head with a bat!

Last summer my uncle and I went to a ball game between the Dodgers and the Padres. The batter slapped a high foul ball toward the third-base stands, which was where we were sitting. The ball was coming right at us! I jumped for the ball and caught it with one hand! But when I jumped I bumped into a woman next to me and knocked a popcorn and lemonade out of her hand. I was really happy about catching the ball, but I was embarrassed about what I had done to the woman. I apologized and went and bought her another popcorn and lemonade.

THINKING ABOUT WHAT YOU HAVE READ

Answer in complete sentences.

1. How did the boy on the left get hit on the head?

   _____

   _____

2. Where, when, and how did the other boy catch the baseball?

   _____

   _____

   _____

3. What happened while he was catching the ball? What happened afterward?

   _____

   _____

   _____

4. Which of the two stories is easiest to understand? Explain.

   _____

   _____

THINKING ABOUT WRITING

Understanding Order in the Personal Narrative

A personal narrative is a story from a person's own life. It is the step-by-step telling of something that really happened. It should have a clear beginning, a middle, and an end.

You probably found the narrative told by the boy who got hit with the baseball a bit hard to follow. Everything is out of order. The events are not told in the order in which they happened.

Following are some of the things that happened to the boy who tells the baseball story. The events are out of order. Number the events in the order in which they occurred. One event has been numbered for you.

_____ **a.** James was taken to the hospital.

___1___ **b.** Ronnie and James were waiting for other players to show up for a baseball game.

_____ **c.** James was hit and knocked out.

_____ **d.** Ronnie threw a ball up in the air and took a swing at it.

_____ **e.** The other kids showed up after James had been hurt.

_____ **f.** Ronnie missed the ball and hit James in the head.

Understanding Order in Sentences

Order is important in narratives. It is also important in the sentences that make up a narrative. For example, the following sentence is put together in a very confusing way. It is not clear whether the little girl or the seagull is wearing an orange dress.

A little girl watched the seagull fly back and forth <u>in an orange dress</u>.

Such a sentence can often be repaired by rearranging the parts.

A little girl <u>in an orange dress</u> watched the seagull fly back and forth.

I.

Rewrite each of the following sentences. Rearrange the parts to make the meaning clear. You will have to change some punctuation and capital letters.

1. The boy tripped over the dog in the new gray suit.

   _____

2. The kids missed what happened who came later.

   _____

3. Hanging from a hook in the garage, Phillip found the wrench.

   _____

   _____

4. In the sink I was washing my clothes.

   _____

5. He spotted a watermelon running down the road.

   _____

Some sentences cannot be repaired simply by rearranging the parts. For example, read the following sentence.

   It hit me in the head, and right into the hospital I went.

This sentence seems to say that the writer was knocked right into the hospital by an object. In order to correct it, we need to get rid of some words, add others, and break the one sentence into two.

   It hit me in the head. I had to be taken to the hospital right away.

II.

Rewrite each of the following sentences. Make whatever changes are needed. The first one is done for you. (The sentences are from real insurance reports filed by drivers.)

1. I was on my way to the doctor with rear-end trouble when my universal joint gave way causing me to have an accident.

   I was on my way to the doctor. My car was having rear-end trouble. The universal joint gave way, causing me to have an accident.

84

2. A truck backed through my windshield into my wife's face.

_____

3. I crashed into a car coming the other way that was parked.

_____

4. I was coming home and drove into the wrong house and smashed into a tree I don't have.

_____

_____

5. I had been driving my car for 30 years when I fell asleep at the wheel and crashed into a tree.

_____

_____

Getting Ready to Write

Soon you will tell a story. Then you will write a story you hear. The following activities will help you get ready.

I.

Many things have happened in your life. The list below will probably trigger some memories. Look through the list. Then circle each thing that once happened to you—and about which you could tell a story. You may add to the list by writing on the lines provided.

I got lost.   I received a special gift.   I got in trouble.   I helped someone.   I got hurt.

I made something.   I was in a contest.   I was in (or at) a sports event.

_____

II.

Now choose one of the events you either circled or wrote in Part I. Think of the story you'd like to tell about the event. Then, on the following lines, list four or five things you want to include in your story. List them in the order in which they happened.

_____

_____

WRITING

A Partner Story

A partner story is just what its name suggests. You get together with a partner and tell each other a story. Then you write the story you were told.

Follow these steps:

1. Think about the incident you chose for Part II on page 85. Decide how to make your story as interesting as possible.

2. Get together with one of your classmates. Ask your classmate to tell you a story about a real event. Take notes as your partner talks.

3. Tell your partner your own true story.

4. Using your notes to help you, write a narrative that tells what happened to your partner. Write it on a separate sheet of paper.

SKILL BUILDING

The Semicolon

The *semicolon* (;) is a mark of punctuation that is stronger than the comma. The semicolon is most often used between two independent clauses *not* joined by a conjunction (*and, but, or, not, for, yet, so*).

Read the following examples. Notice that a conjunction and a comma are used in the first sentence. In the second sentence, in which the conjunction is missing, a semicolon is used instead of the comma.

EXAMPLE 1:

A human needs only 3 pounds of food a day, but an elephant needs about 300 pounds.

A human needs only 3 pounds of food a day; an elephant needs about 300 pounds.

EXAMPLE 2:

Mount Logan is Canada's highest mountain, and Mt. Fairweather is its second highest.

Mount Logan is Canada's highest mountain; Mt. Fairweather is its second highest.

I.

Each of the following statements requires a semicolon. Read the statements and add the semicolons.

1. I have only one tent pole it won't be enough.

2. I brought some wood it was heavy.

3. I lost my glasses I can't find them anywhere.

4. I washed your sleeping bag it shrank.

5. You use that on the trip I'll use yours.

II.

In the illustration that follows, write an appropriate sentence in each loop. Each sentence must have a semicolon.

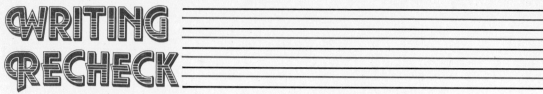

WRITING RECHECK

THINKING ABOUT WRITING

1. Get together again with your partner. Exchange papers. Look for the following items in your partner's paragraph.

    a. Does your partner list all the main points you told him or her? On the following lines, write any that are left out.

       _____

       _____

    b. Are there any errors in the details your partner wrote? If so, explain them below.

       _____

       _____

    c. Are the events written in the order in which they happened? If not, explain where the order is mixed up. (Be sure to ask yourself whether you told the events in the right order.)

       _____

       _____

    d. Are there any sentences written in a confusing way? If so, copy them below. Make any corrections that are needed.

       _____

       _____

SKILL BUILDING

2. Have you, in any place in your narrative, used two sentences that might be combined as one, using a semicolon? If so, rewrite them as a single sentence on your paper.

3. Study your partner's writing. Put a check mark (✔) in the blank in front of any of the following problems that you find. Discuss with your partner ways to correct each problem.

_____ misused homophones   _____ incorrect end-of-sentence punctuation

_____ run-on sentences   _____ incorrect use of commas and semicolons

_____ sentence fragments   _____ capitalization errors

I MEAN BUSINESS

On October 25, Wilma Wirtle, Sandy Lipps, and Iona Kastel saw this ad in *Fun Fashions,* their favorite magazine.

Excited, the three girls ordered matching jackets, in the zebra-stripe print. A few weeks later, when they received their jackets, they were terribly disappointed. All the jackets were the wrong size, and they were metallic blond, not zebra stripe. Batteries were not included. Even when the girls used their own batteries, the electric zippers did not work.

Wilma, Sandy, and Iona each wrote a letter to Elektro Jackets.

8273 Klikker Street
Wary, Indiana 46809

November 18, 1986

Elektro Jackets, Inc.
12345 6th Street
Bongo, CA 91726

Dear Elektro Jackets:

On October 25, I ordered a Bunnysloper ski jacket in the zebra print, size 8. The jacket I received was a size 16 in the metallic blond. In addition, the zipper did not work, nor were batteries included.

Your advertisement in *Fun Fashions* magazine promises "no risk—money-back guarantee." I am hereby asking for a refund in the amount of $58.99. I, of course, will return the jacket.

Thank you for your attention.

Sincerely yours,

Sandy Lipps

November 17

Electro Jackets, Inc.
12345 6th Street
Bongo, CA 91726

Hi there!

My name is Wilma, and I just love *Fun Fashions* magazine. I read it every week. But now I'll never read it again, 'cause I'm so upset!

Why am I upset? Well, I'll tell you. I ordered a jacket, but it came in the wrong color and size. And the electric zipper didn't work. Even my uncle Wilbert, who is very good with zippers, couldn't get it to work. And no batteries arrived in the package either!

Have a heart and send me my money back. Pretty please, with sugar on top!

Love,

Wilma Wintle

4864 Tellso Ave.
Wary, Indiana 46809

November 17, 1986

Elektro Jackets, Inc.
12345 6th Street
Bongo, CA 91726

Dear Elektro Jackets:

Who do you think you're dealing with? Dudes like you really rub me the wrong way!

I saw a jacket advertised. It was in *Fun Fashions* magazine. I ordered the Bunnysloper ski jacket. I ordered zebra-stripe print. I got metallic blond. You said batteries included. I got not batteries. The zipper does not work. It is the wrong size. I ordered a size 12. You sent a 6.

Send me my money, if you know what's good for you! I won't take this from anyone!

Sincerely,

Iona Kastel

THINKING ABOUT WHAT YOU HAVE READ

Answer in complete sentences.

1. Elektro Jackets wouldn't be able to send Wilma Wirtle her money back. Why?

    _____

    _____

    _____

2. What is there about the form and tone of Wilma's letter that are unbusinesslike? Explain.

    _____

    _____

    _____

3. Sandy Lipps's letter is more businesslike. Compare its form and tone with Wilma's.

    _____

    _____

    _____

    _____

4. What is the tone of Iona Kastel's letter? Do you think the tone is appropriate? Explain.

    _____

    _____

    _____

5. Iona includes most of the necessary information. But does she do so as effectively as Sandy? Compare Iona's style of writing with Sandy's.

    _____

    _____

    _____

6. Wilma's letter includes a lot of unnecessary information. Underline those phrases and sentences in her letter that you think are unnecessary.

THINKING ABOUT WRITING

The Business Letter—Form and Content

Below is the correct form for a business letter. The *heading* has the sender's address and the date. The *inside address* includes the name of the person and the name and address of the company to which you are writing. The *salutation* is the greeting.

The body of a business letter is your message. The first paragraph should state the problem or the situation. The second paragraph should state what you want done.

The last two elements of a business letter are the *closing* and the *signature.* The closing should be courteous and formal. The signature should include your whole name.

Heading { 18921 Surfboard Boulevard
Miami, Florida 33054
April 19, 1986

Mr. Clyde Sides
Playwrong Record Company
11129 Rockout Street
Bandville, Mississippi   10000 } **Inside Address**

Dear Mr. Sides: } **Salutation**

Your company, Playwrong Records, recently released a song entitled "Chicken-Walkin' Mama." It is sung by Big Abe and the Lincolns.

Since I cannot find this record in my area, I would like to order a copy from your catalog. Enclosed is a check for $2.50 for "Chicken-Walkin' Mama." This is item number 8574-L in your catalog. } **Body**

Closing { Sincerely yours,

Signature { *Alma Matter*

I.

The following letter is incomplete. Compare it with the sample letter on page 92. Then fill in the missing information and punctuation.

9587 Barker Road

Los Angeles California

March 14

Ethel Gasoween

Sales Manager

Comfy-Wumfy Doggy Raincoat Co.

1919 Canine Avenue

Detroit   48123

Ms Gasoween

   I have a toy poodle named Wifferkins. Sometimes he is a naughty boy and goes out in the rain. I would like to order a size 2, red doggy raincoat for my dog. My husband thinks yellow would be cuter, but I disagree with him because he is always wrong. The catalog number is 4675, and the price is $49.85.

   Enclosed is a check in that amount. Please hurry, because Wifferkins is really looking forward to getting his new raincoat!

Mabel Lurch

A good business letter should contain only necessary information. Remember, you are doing business, not chatting on paper with a friend.

II.

Reread Mabel Lurch's letter. Cross out those phrases and sentences that are unnecessary or otherwise inappropriate for a business letter.

Getting Ready to Write

Soon you are going to write a letter requesting that a mail-order company send you a pair of pajamas. The following will help you get ready to write.

I.

Following are all the facts you will need in your letter. There are also a lot of unnecessary facts. Underline those facts you will include in your letter.

1. The name of the company is Cushy-Sleepers, Inc.

2. The address of the company is 85767 Regal Street, Jamesville, Pennsylvania 15225.

3. The pajamas are for your little brother Sammy.

4. Mr. Edward Adams is the sales manager of the company.

5. Sammy sometimes kicks his blankets off in his sleep.

6. You heard about Cushy-Sleepers from your aunt who lives in Jamesville, Pennsylvania.

7. The catalog number is 76586-T.

8. You want a red blanket sleeper with the clowns-and-drums pattern.

9. You want a size 6.

10. If they don't have red in stock, you will take a blue—but no other color.

11. The blanket sleeper costs $12.50, including tax.

12. There is also a $1.50 postage and handling fee.

13. You are enclosing a check for $14.00.

II.

Give the information requested in each item that follows.

1. Write your address on the first _____

   two lines at the right. _____

   Write today's date on the third line _____

   (The above information is your heading.)

2. Using the list of information in Part I, write an inside address for your letter. This is the person and company to which you are writing.

_____

_____

_____

_____

_____

3. Write a closing and a signature. _____

_____

WRITING

A Business Letter

On a separate sheet of paper, write a business letter ordering the blanket sleeper. Use your answers to "Getting Ready to Write" (pages 94 and 95) to guide you. Be sure to state what you want done.

SKILL BUILDING

The Colon

The *colon* (:) is a punctuation mark with three main uses.

1. Use a colon to introduce and direct attention to something that will follow.
   He bought the following items: a towel, a razor, soap, and shaving cream.

2. Use a colon after the salutation in a business letter.
   Dear Mr. Wigglesworth:

3. Use a colon between hours and minutes.
   7:48 P.M.

Ten colons are missing from the following business letter. Read the letter.
Then go back and add the colons where they belong.

85838 Wearnot Lane
Girlsy, Idaho 83645
May 27, 1985

Mr. Willy Nilly
General Manager
Tootsie Shoe Company
46736 Highboot Street
Podos, Oregon   96764

Dear Mr. Nilly

I recently purchased the following items from your company by mail high-heeled tennis shoes, air-conditioned combat boots, self-propelled jogging shoes, and Roger Rabbit bedroom slippers. I am very disappointed in these products.

The heels on my high-heeled tennis shoes broke off the first day I wore them. I tried to fix them by doing these things gluing the heels with rubber cement, nailing them with rubber nails, and melting the parts together with a blow torch. Nothing worked.

Next we come to my air-conditioned combat boots. At 9 30 A.M. last Thursday the air conditioner jammed on high. Before I could get the boots off, my feet were frostbitten! The doctors had to do the following to save my poor tootsies breathe on them, rub them, soak them in hot alligator milk, and hold them over a camp fire. As a result, this is what my feet are like now sore, bruised, itchy, and smelly.

Then there's my self-propelled jogging shoes. I don't know whether they work, due to the following fact I wear a size 16, and you sent me a size 4!

My Roger Rabbit bedroom slippers were worst of all. They were used! Here are just some of the reasons why I am sure of this there are scuff marks on the soles, there are food stains on the tops, and there was a dirty sock still stuffed in one of them.

I want my money back ($164.37) for these shoes. If you do not send it to me, I will have to take some sort of action against your company. The following ideas come to mind suing you, sending a letter about you to the president of the United States, or saying mean things about you to my friends.

As you can tell, I mean business. Return my money by 12 59 P.M. on Tuesday of next week, or I will have to take stronger measures.

Sincerely yours,

Richard Lizardson

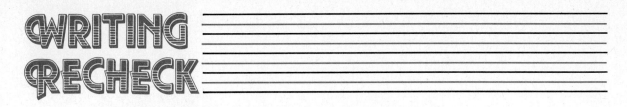

THINKING ABOUT WRITING

1. Compare your business letter with the example letter shown on page 92. Study your heading, inside address, salutation, body, closing, and signature. Correct any errors you find.

2. Are there any unnecessary phrases or sentences in your letter? If so, cross them out.

3. Are there any words, phrases, or sentences that express strong personal feelings? Is there any slang? If so, remove these words or phrases from your letter.

4. Are there any places where you used a series of short, choppy sentences? Can these be combined into one longer sentence? If so, redo these sentences on the lines below.

_____

_____

_____

_____

_____

_____

_____

_____

_____

SKILL BUILDING

5. Check your usage of the following punctuation marks: period, question mark, exclamation point, and colon. Correct any errors you find.

HOLLYWOOD— SUMMING UP

The average American will go to the movies 350 times during a lifetime. The average American will also spend roughly 20 years of his or her life watching television. About a third of this time will be devoted to watching movies.

A scene from *The African Queen*, starring Katharine Hepburn and Humphrey Bogart.

Most of the movies you see are quickly forgotten. Look at the photo on page 98. It is a scene from a famous movie. Have you ever seen it? If so, could you describe what happens in this story?

A summary of this movie follows.

The Queen of Movies

The African Queen is an old movie, but it is a great one. It is what most people would call a movie "classic." The main characters are Charlie Allnutt, played by Humphrey Bogart, and Rose Sayer, played by Katharine Hepburn.

The story takes place in central Africa during World War I. The Germans have swept through the area. Most people have been killed or have run away.

Charlie Allnutt comes steaming down the river in a run-down old boat called the *African Queen.* He stops at an English mission, which has been attacked and is in ruins. The only person there is a missionary named Rose Sayer. Her brother has died. Charlie and Rose head down the river.

Charlie is a sloppy, easy-going man. And he is not very brave. His plan is to take the boat to an island downriver, where he and Rose can hide from the Germans. Then they can either wait there until the war is over or, if they are lucky, be rescued by the English.

Rose is a plain-looking, upright, and patriotic woman. She is not interested in Charlie's plan. She wants to fight, to strike a blow for England. She wants to steam downriver past a German fort, shoot the rapids, and reach a lake where she knows a German gunboat is prowling. Her plan is to use the explosives on board the *African Queen* to blow up the German vessel.

At first, Charlie thinks the idea is crazy. But, little by little, he falls in love with Rose, and she with him. Finally, they decide to carry out Rose's plan.

Their voyage is a terrible ordeal. As the *African Queen* chugs down the river, Charlie and Rose are plagued by insects, leeches, heat, and malaria. They are almost shipwrecked on the rapids. As they race past the German fort, they are shot at with rifles and cannons.

Then things get worse. They get stuck in a swamp. For miles, they have to drag the *African Queen* through shallow, jungle waters.

Finally, they reach the lake and sight the German gunboat. They rig up a torpedo on the bow of the *African Queen.* With this, they plan to ram the German boat in a suicidal attack.

A storm develops and sinks the *Queen* before the attack can be made. Rose and Charlie are picked up from the water and taken aboard the German ship. The Germans prepare to hang them.

About to be hanged, Charlie spots the sunken *African Queen.* It is floating underwater toward the German ship. The *Queen's* torpedo rams into the ship. Charlie and Rose leap overboard as the ship explodes.

Rose and Charlie find each other in the water. They are filled with excitement and hope. From the way they act, you know they will reach safety. You know their love for each other will only grow.

The movie *The African Queen* is one of the great movies of all time. I could watch it ten times without tiring of it. I recommend it to anyone who loves a good adventure story.

THINKING ABOUT WHAT YOU HAVE READ

Answer in complete sentences.

1. What information is given in the opening paragraph of the summary?

   _____

   _____

   _____

2. The summary tells what happens in *The African Queen* in the same order in which the events are shown in the movie. Is this an effective way to go about telling what happens? Explain.

   _____

   _____

   _____

3. The summary tells what the characters are like. What is Charlie like? What is Rose like?

   _____

   _____

   _____

   _____

4. What problems are described in the summary?

   _____

   _____

   _____

5. The summary tells the setting. Where does the story take place? When does it take place? How is the setting important to the story? Explain.

   _____

   _____

   _____

   _____

THINKING ABOUT WRITING

Paragraphing and Structure

A piece of writing has to be divided into paragraphs. The paragraphs should be arranged in a logical, orderly manner. Without paragraphs, or with the paragraphs in the wrong order, a piece of writing has as little appeal as a poorly made movie.

The paragraphs in the following selection are out of order. Read them carefully. Then show the order in which they belong by writing a number in the blank. The first one has been done for you.

The Real Way To Make A Movie

_____ **a.** After Ojinaga, more battles were fought. For the cameras, everything had to happen during the day. Thus Villa was told to delay all fighting until 9:00 A.M., when the sun was up. Then, at 4:00 P.M., when darkness set in, the fighting had to end.

_____ **b.** Villa accepted the offer. Aitken moved his film company into Mexico. Director Walsh began looking for locations for battles to take place.

_____ **c.** What happened to the movie itself? Director Walsh brought it back to the studios in the U.S. Incredibly, those who saw it thought the battle scenes were dull and phony-looking! Most of the movie had to be reshot on a studio lot.

_____ **d.** There were other problems besides lighting. Sometimes the soldiers on horseback rode too fast for the cameras to catch the action; the soldiers were told to slow down. More than once a battle had to be stopped until the cameras could be moved to a new angle. And if a battle scene went badly on film, it had to be fought again!

_____ **e.** It all began in 1914 when Harry Aitken, president of Mutual Film Corporation, decided to make a feature film called _The Life of General Villa_. Aitken met with Villa in Mexico. He offered to pay Villa $25,000 if the soldier would allow real battles to be filmed. But Aitken's director, Raoul Walsh, would tell Villa when and how to attack.

___1___ **f.** One thing you probably don't know about Pancho Villa is that he was the star of an American-made movie. And the movie was one of the strangest ever made. In it, Villa conducted part of a real revolution, according to a prepared movie script!

_____ **g.** Walsh decided that a town called Ojinaga would be a good place for the first battle scene. Villa agreed and prepared to attack. But the cameras had not yet been set up. An angry Villa had to hold up the battle until all was ready for the moviemakers. The delay allowed the enemy time to reinforce, but Villa overran them anyway.

Getting Ready to Write

Soon you will write a summary of a movie. The movie may be one that your teacher selects for you to watch in class. Or it may be one you watch on TV as homework. Your teacher will tell you. After the movie has been selected, follow these steps.

I.

Notetaking

As you watch the movie, take notes. Make sure you get all of the following on paper:

a.   the title of the movie.

b.   the names of the stars and the names of the characters they play.

c.   a description of the most important events that occur in the story.

d.   a description of what the characters are like.

e.   the setting of the movie.

f.   a description of the main conflicts in the story.

II.

Organizing Your Information
1.   In your introductory paragraph, include all the following information:
     a.   the name of the movie.
     b.   the type of movie (For example, is it science fiction, romance, or adventure?).
     c.   the names of the stars and the names of the characters they play.

2.   On a separate sheet of paper, write a rough draft of your introductory paragraph.

3.   Study your notes. On your paper, make a list of five or six of the most important things that happen in the movie. Write them in the order in which they occur in the movie. This list is the framework for your summary. That is, each item will be the topic of a separate paragraph. Be sure to include information about the setting of the movie. Also include important conflicts.

4.   What is your opinion of the movie? Would you recommend that others see it? Why or why not? Answer these questions on your paper. Use this information to develop the concluding paragraph of your summary.

WRITING

A Movie Summary

On a separate sheet of paper, write a summary of the movie you watched. Use your notes and your answers to "Getting Ready to Write" (page 102) to guide you.

SKILL BUILDING

Parentheses

Parentheses ( ) are used to enclose various kinds of extra or clarifying information. For example . . .

> *The Book of Firsts* (page 65) says that the first animal star
> was the dog Rover, hero of the 1905 box-office hit *Rescued*.

Read the sentences that follow and the parenthetical elements to the right of them. Then, on a sheet of paper, rewrite each sentence, placing the parenthetical element where it belongs. The first one has been done for you.

1. *The African Queen* is one of the ten most often shown movies on television.

   (starring Humphrey Bogart and Katharine Hepburn)

   The African Queen (starring Humphrey Bogart and Katharine Hepburn) is one of the ten most often shown movies on television.

2. The beginning of *The Wizard of Oz* is in black-and-white; most of the rest is in color.

   (the first 18 minutes)

3. In the movie *All Quiet on the Western Front,* only ex-soldiers acted in the battle scenes.

   (2,000 of them)

4. Actor Douglas Fairbanks was once offered $1 million if he would teach gymnastics to a wealthy teenager, Thomas Rhodes.

   (who was an expert gymnast)

103

5. Boston newspapers ran an ad in 1970 for Walt Disney's *Peter Pan,* which carried an "G" rating.

(children under 18 are admitted without a parent or guardian)

6. Andy Warhol's movie *Sleep* features close-ups of a man getting eight hours sleep.

(which is, appropriately, eight hours in length)

7. The city of Hollywood was founded by a temperance society.

(a group against the drinking of alcohol)

8. Grace Kelly starred in *High Noon, Rear Window,* and *Dial M for Murder.*

(who became Princess Grace of Monaco)

THINKING ABOUT WRITING

1. Is your summary broken into paragraphs that present ideas in a clear and logical way? If not, rewrite your summary. Ask your teacher for guidance.

2. Make sure the first line of each paragraph is indented.

3. In movies we see cause-and-effect relationships. As homework, watch a movie on TV. Make a list of five cause-and-effect relationships you see. You may want to look back at pages 74 through 75 to refresh your memory of cause-and-effect.

SKILL BUILDING

4. Recheck your usage of the following punctuation marks in your summary: period, question mark, exclamation point, comma, semicolon, colon, and parentheses. Make any changes or corrections necessary.

5. Check for the following in your summary: fragments, incorrect pronoun case, problems in subject-verb agreement, run-ons, homophone errors. Correct any mistakes you find.

OBJECTIVE POETRY

A dog waits for its master. A girl helps her younger brother cross the street. A police officer sits quietly and sips a cup of coffee. These are examples of subjects for *objective poems*. An **objective poem** is simply an observation. The writer describes something without expressing a personal opinion.

Objective poems are written in *free verse*. **Free verse** is poetry that has no regular pattern or rhythm. The lines usually are not all the same length, and there is no rhyme scheme.

The following objective poems were written by students.

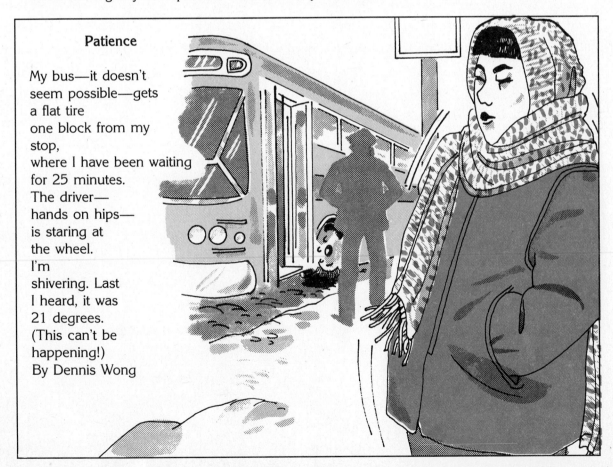

Patience

My bus—it doesn't
seem possible—gets
a flat tire
one block from my
stop,
where I have been waiting
for 25 minutes.
The driver—
hands on hips—
is staring at
the wheel.
I'm
shivering. Last
I heard, it was
21 degrees.
(This can't be
happening!)
By Dennis Wong

The Necklace

A red-haired girl
sits
at the dinner
table. She
has no intention
of eating
her peas. Instead,
she makes a green
pearl necklace out of
them—
on her plate.

By Deborah Holt

Sleep

The old dog
lies on a step
watching the
young
dog run about and
bark.
The old dog
yawns,
puts his head
on
his paws,
and sleeps.

By Mark Hastings

Laughter

A boy in a hockey uniform is
walking
down
the
street. He
hears
someone laugh.
He turns around,
wondering if
the person was laughing
at him.

By Victor Torres

Meow

The spoiled kitten waits
for her mistress to
rub her tummy.
She meows pitifully,
but no one hears her.
She moves
next to her mistress's
feet
and begins to purr.

By Jennifer Sara

Thoughts

The teacher is
sitting at her desk
waiting for the
students
to finish their assignment.
She has a far-off look
in her eyes
as though she is
in
a special world
all her
own.

By Brenda Lott

106

THINKING ABOUT WHAT YOU HAVE READ

Answer in complete sentences.

1. Which of the poems did you enjoy most? Explain.

   _____

   _____

   _____

   _____

2. Reread the poem by Victor Torres. Have you ever thought someone was laughing at you, but you really weren't sure? Explain.

   _____

   _____

   _____

3. Take a second look at the poem by Mark Hastings. What might have been going through the old dog's mind? Explain.

   _____

   _____

   _____

4. In the poem by Dennis Wong, what do you think is the importance of the bus breaking down one block from his stop? If it were a mile away, how would the poem be different? Explain.

   _____

   _____

   _____

5. Deborah Holt could have said the girl "makes a circle of peas on her plate." Instead, she said she "makes a green pearl necklace." Which is the better description? Explain.

   _____

   _____

   _____

   _____

THINKING ABOUT WRITING

Writing Vivid Descriptions

A good piece of writing comes alive on the page. The writer makes you see what is being described—and makes you hear it, smell it, taste it, and touch it.

I.

In each poem that follows, some words and phrases are underlined. Identify the sense to which each underlined word or phrase most appeals. On the lines provided, write *see, hear, smell, taste,* or *touch.*

Dad opened the oven door
and removed the apple pies
he had made.
The room was filled with
the sharp-sweet scent
of cinnamon.   1. _____

The boy stuck a
chunk of ham
into his mouth.
For a moment
it hung there like
a huge red tongue.   2. _____
Then he
slurped and pulled   3. _____
it inward
and began to chew.

A kid
wearing dark-green tennis shoes   4. _____
walked down
Missouri Street,
singing softly.   5. _____
He aimed one tennis-shoed foot
at
a tin can
and sent it
clattering
and rattling   6. _____
down
Missouri Street.

A good description also creates *spatial order.* It helps the reader see where all things are in relation to one another. Words and phrases such as *on the right, against,* and *in between* create spatial order.

II.

Write a word or a phrase of your choice in each blank in the following poem. Use words that create spatial order. The first one has been done as an example.

The spaniel lazily plopped

forward on _____ the soft grass.
He turned on his side as
a butterfly floated

_____.

The spaniel raised
his head and

looked _____ as
the butterfly settled

_____ on a branch. Bored,

the spaniel rolled _____

his _____ side and stared
into space.

III.

A description also shows mood or feeling. It might show joy, anger, sadness, or contentment. Read the following poem. Think about what mood it conveys. Notice the changes in mood from the beginning to the end. When you are through reading, answer the questions on page 110.

The young girl,
A champion gymnast,
giggled and
clapped her hands.
She was confident she
would win the prize.
But she didn't.
And very slowly,
head hanging,
she walked back to where
her parents
were
standing
and
watching,
holding back their tears,
trying not to show
their disappointment.

Answer in complete sentences.

1. What is the mood at the beginning of the poem?

    _____

2. What is the mood at the end of the poem?

    _____

3. How does the change in mood make what happens at the end of the poem even sadder? Explain.

    _____

    _____

Getting Ready to Write

Soon you will write some *objective poems.* The following will help you get ready to write.

An **objective poem** is based on something you observe. Take time out and watch as life goes by. Note details of sight, sound, taste, smell, and touch. Observe spatial relationships. Become aware of moods and feelings.

Sit somewhere and observe what is going on. This may be in a classroom, in your home, at a park—anywhere. If you are in a park, you might observe a game of frisbee. You might look closely at some butterflies or at a dog chasing a ball. Or you might note what is going on at a construction site across the street, or watch a traffic jam on the corner.

On a separate sheet of paper, take notes about what you see. Be sure to make your notes detailed and specific. You will need these notes in order to write your poems.

Objective Poems

An objective poem is a special type of descriptive writing. There are three important differences between an objective poem and a prose description. First, the poem is very condensed. It tells what happens in as few words as possible. Second, the language is chosen to create a particular emotional response. Third, the poem is not written in paragraph-form across the page. The lines break wherever the writer thinks it is best.

Take another look at the poems on pages 105–106. Use them as examples of what objective poems look like. Next, read what you wrote in "Getting Ready to Write." It should give you ideas for poem topics. Then, on a separate sheet of paper, write two or three objective poems.

SKILL BUILDING

The Hyphen

The hyphen **(-)** has five main uses:

1. to join some compound nouns.
   free-for-all   brother-in-law   double-dealer

2. to combine two or more words used as a single adjective.
   easy-going   matter-of-fact   fair-haired   long-standing

3. to join the parts of compound numbers.
   forty-five   ninety-three

4. to signal the division of a word at the end of a printed line.

   As the sailor walked on deck, he saw huge clouds pushed by a tremen-dous wind.

   (Note: When a word has to be broken at the end of a line, always place the hyphen between two syllables: *tremen-dous,* not *tr-emendous.*)

5. to join some prefixes to a base word.
   self-discipline   mid-life   pro-American

I.

Place hyphens where they are needed in the following sentences.

1. After giving her talk on pre Columbian art, the long haired teacher made an ultra fast exit from the stage.

2. The soft spoken boy wearing the corduroy pants shocked everybody in the stadium by heaving the shot put almost thirty four feet.

3. The stoop backed man looked at her and said, "You're the most honest, open minded, self giving person I know."

4. He had a long handled wooden back scratcher he said he had purchased when he was vacationing in Spain.

Read the poems on pages 105 and 106. Circle any hyphenated words you find.

The Dash

The most interesting thing about the *dash* **(—)** is that it can be used in place of several other punctuation marks. It can be used in place of . . .

THE SEMICOLON:

> Take my jacket; I'm not cold.
> Take my jacket—I'm not cold.

THE COLON:

> You should bring the three tools: the hacksaw, the screwdriver, and the wrench.
> You should bring the three tools—the hacksaw, the screwdriver, and the wrench.

THE PARENTHESES:

> The three dogs (Spike, Judo, and Ringo) followed me up the hill.
> The three dogs—Spike, Judo, and Ringo—followed me up the hill.

Most often, though, the dash is used to indicate a sudden shift, break, or interruption of thought:

> Joe Finkel's mother—or maybe it was his aunt—won first place in the contest.

In the following sentences, place dashes where they are needed. If another punctuation mark can be used in place of the dash, write it in the box following the sentence.

> **EXAMPLE:** His good qualities are many ‾ patience, understanding, and
> love.   ∧

1. I dropped the rock into the well I never heard it hit. ☐

2. Only three people Bobby, Mel, and Stephanie were at the party. ☐

3. Some of my tools my saw, my drill, and my hammer are missing. ☐

4. I saw your cat or maybe it was mine in the tree. ☐

5. We can't drive there the road is blocked. ☐

THINKING ABOUT WRITING

1. Look over the objective poems you wrote. Which of your poems do you like best? Explain.

   _____

   _____

   _____

2. Underline any words or phrases in your poems that appeal to the senses (sight, sound, taste, touch, or smell).

3. For each poem you wrote, think of *one* word that would describe its mood. Write that word below the poem.

SKILL BUILDING

4. Did you use any hyphens in your poems? If so, circle them.

5. Review your use of the following punctuation marks: period, question mark, exclamation point, comma, semicolon, colon, parentheses, dash, hyphen. Make any changes or corrections necessary.

6. Check for the following in your poems: fragments, incorrect pronoun cases, problems in subject-verb agreement, homophone errors. Correct any mistakes you find.

THE THINGS PEOPLE SAY

Sometimes a person says something to you that you remember for a long time. The comment may upset you and make you feel sad. Or it may be a comment that makes you feel very good.

Sandy Laurence of Wichita, Kansas, was asked to record a memorable comment and her response to that comment. She was given two loops. In one loop (below, left), she wrote what someone once said. In the other loop (below, right), Sandy wrote her response to those words.

After filling in the loops, Sandy wrote a brief composition describing what was said to her, how she reacted, and what happened later in relation to the comment.

Sandy, basketball is a sport for boys. I know you are tall, but that doesn't mean you have to be a basketball player. Don't do things that aren't feminine. Be a lady. Forget basketball. Do this, if you love me.

Basketball is as much for girls as for boys. I love the sport. Someday I may be really terrific at it. And loving you has nothing to do with it. I can't believe you would even say such a thing. You just don't seem to understand that there are things I have to do in my life that are all my own.

About two years ago my mother told me to quit the basketball team, that basketball wasn't for girls. I was really hurt by the comment, and I told her so. I told her I intended to keep playing.

Well, I did keep playing. In fact, last semester my school's team won the regional championship. In the championship game I scored 18 points, had 9 rebounds, and blocked 2 shots.

And guess who was at the game? My mom! She was really happy for me. Her attitude has changed a lot since she made that comment to me a couple of years ago.

THINKING ABOUT WHAT YOU HAVE READ

Answer in complete sentences.

1. Why was Sandy upset by her mother's comment that Sandy—and girls in general—should not play basketball?

_____

_____

_____

2. Why, do you think, did Sandy continue playing?

_____

_____

_____

3. Two years later, how had Sandy's mother's attitude changed?

_____

_____

_____

4. Has anyone ever told you not to do something and you did it anyway? Briefly explain what happened.

_____

_____

_____

_____

THINKING ABOUT WRITING

Intent and Transition

Read the following two paragraphs about sports. Which one contains mostly facts? Which expresses the personal opinion of the writer?

Men think they are the only ones who can excel in sports. They think they should be on the field of play while women sit in the stands and watch them. That is nonsense! I say, women belong in athletics as much as men do.

In ancient Greece, women were not allowed to participate in the Olympic Games. They were forbidden even to watch the games. According to a law of the time, any woman caught watching would be taken up a mountain and thrown to her death from a cliff! It is not known if this was just a threat or if it was actually done.

In the first paragraph the writer uses a *subjective* style. The writer freely expresses feelings and opinions. (An **opinion** is an idea that cannot be proved.) Such a style is appropriate in a friendly letter, in informal compositions, and in describing personal experiences.

The second paragraph is an example of an *objective* style of writing. Here the writer states the facts without sharing any personal feelings. (A **fact** is a statement that can be proved through evidence.) Formal compositions, some business letters, and reports usually require an objective rather than a subjective style.

Read each of the following sentences. If the style seems *subjective*, write *S* beside the number. If it seems *objective*, write *O*.

_____ 1. At one time, male tennis players wore long pants.

_____ 2. One would look foolish playing tennis in long pants.

_____ 3. I've been hurt several times playing football.

_____ 4. Frederick, Prince of Wales, was killed in 1751 when he was struck by a cricket ball.

_____ 5. Football is a barbaric sport that should be outlawed.

_____ 6. Hugh Daly became a major-league pitcher despite the fact he had only one arm.

_____ 7. The soldiers of ancient Rome played field hockey.

_____ 8. My father taught me how to play golf.

In a piece of writing, a **transition** is a word or a phrase that smoothly connects one idea to another. It relates a preceding topic to one that follows.

Such words and phrases as *however, in that case,* and *secondly* can help a writer make easy transitions. They can help the writer move smoothly from one sentence to another.

To the paragraph that follows, add the *italicized* words and phrases (where they belong) to make smooth transitions between sentences.

Don't forget to add the commas which must follow such phrases.

In fact,   Alone,   For example,

Some American heroes were not exactly everything we have long believed they were. _____ Paul Revere was not alone when he went on his famous midnight ride to warn the colonists that "The Redcoats are coming!" A man named William Dawes rode with Revere. Dawes started out before Revere and rode longer. Dawes did the whole job right, while Revere got sidetracked and never finished his ride. _____ toward the end of the ride, Revere was captured by the British. _____ Dawes rode on into the night to finish the brave task for which his companion would get all the credit.

Getting Ready to Write

On page 118 you will write a composition about something important that someone once said to you. The following activities will help you get ready to write.

1. Read the following list of characteristics, interests, and goals. Think of each one in relation to you. Underline those about which you recall someone making a comment to you.

    Someone has commented on my: intelligence   clothing   physical build

    hair   posture   eyes   athletic ability   future   manner of talking

    career goals   school work   way of treating others   personality   parents

2. Circle the item about which the most memorable comment was made.

3. On the following lines, write the name of the person who made the comment. Then write one *objective* sentence about the person. Next, write one *subjective* sentence about the person.

> **EXAMPLE:** (objective): Ron lived next door.
> (subjective): Ron was the rudest boy on our block.

A Composition

Imagine that the mouth at the left belongs to someone who said something to you—something that you will always remember. In that loop, write what the person said to you. Then imagine that you are the person at the right. In that loop, write what, if anything, you replied to the other person. When you are through, move on to the second part of the writing assignment.

Now, on a separate sheet of paper, write a brief composition. Begin by explaining the comment that was made to you. Explain the circumstances. Give the name of the person who made the comment. Then, in the next paragraph, explain your reaction. Tell what, if anything, you said in response. Tell how you felt. In the last paragraph, tell what happened later as a result of the comment.

SKILL BUILDING

Quotation Marks

The most common use of quotation marks (" ") is to show the beginning and the end of the actual words that somebody said or wrote.

> **EXAMPLE:** My brother looked at me and said, "You really have a strange sense of humor."

I.

Place quotation marks around what is said in the following sentences.

1. You are a beautiful person, said Patty.

2. May I have a bite of your sandwich? the doctor asked.

3. Mr. Johnson, my history teacher, handed me my test and said, You got an *A*; I got the highest mark in the class.

4. You'd be a great soccer player, said coach Green, if only you would train.

5. Dave looked at me and said, Someday you're going to be famous.

6. She read my story, put it down, and said, And you really think you're going to be a writer?

7. Without a doubt, said my grandfather, you're going to make your mark in the world someday!

8. He glanced over at me and said, Who'd dance with him?

9. A man I didn't know walked up to me and said, Those are really great-looking boots.

10. You're only 16—you're too young to go on dates, my mother said.

11. I don't know why I'm laughing, she told me.

12. I asked her, Was it something that I said?

A **direct quotation** is the speaker's or writer's original words. These words are identified by quotation marks. An **indirect quotation** sums up someone else's words. An indirect quotation does not take quotation marks.

> **EXAMPLE:** (direct quotation): He said, "You may have it."
> (indirect quotation): He said that you may have it.

II.

Change each of the following direct quotations into an indirect quotation. You may have to change some words or change the word order slightly in some cases.

1. Tommy said, "Somebody stole the radio."

   _____

2. "It wasn't fair," she yelled.

   _____

3. "Don't you touch it," she warned me.

   _____

4. "It's the most beautiful place in the world," Sandy said.

   _____

5. Donna said, "Jack promised to be here."

   _____

THINKING ABOUT WRITING

1. Reread your composition about something someone has said to you. Underline any phrases or sentences that express an opinion.

2. Are any of your sentences constructed in a confusing way? If so, rewrite them.

3. Is your composition divided into paragraphs? If not, rewrite it. Create paragraph divisions as you write.

SKILL BUILDING

4. In your composition, recheck your use of the following punctuation marks: period, question mark, exclamation point, comma, semicolon, colon, parentheses, dash, hyphen, quotation marks. Make any necessary changes or corrections.

5. Check for the following in your composition: fragments, incorrect pronoun case, run-ons, homophone errors. Correct any mistakes you find.

THE FICTIONAL TWIST

Many stories end with a twist—a final touch that makes the reader see what went before in a new light. The story that follows, "The Ring," ends this way. As you read it, try to figure out the ending—the twist—before it comes.

The Ring

I had a strange dream the other night. At least that is what I think it was.

I dreamed I was in a dark forest. It was just before dawn, and everything around me was cold and damp and gray. I was alone and afraid.

Suddenly I saw a girl. She was running, and she seemed terrified. Her hair was long and blond and flowed behind her. She was wearing a long dress that seemed out of the past, and she was barefoot.

The girl stopped running. She had seen me. Out of breath, she walked slowly over to where I was standing. Her beautiful face was filled with fear.

"Please, sir, you must help me," cried the girl, in an oddly accented voice.

"What's wrong? Who are you? And where am I?" I asked, all in one breath.

"I am Gwendolyn of Fawnsdale castle."

"Castle?" I stammered. "You're from a castle? What year is this?"

"Oh, please, sir, there is no time for jesting," cried Gwendolyn. "It is the year 1147." She grabbed my hand. "The Serpent of Jebua pursues me, and it is near!"

"1147? Castles? The Serpent of Jebua?" I blurted. Somehow I had stumbled into some sort of medieval dreamworld.

"Oh, by all that's holy!" screamed Gwendolyn, pointing. "There it is!"

The most horrible thing I had ever seen was slithering toward us. It was a snake, but it had a human face. Its long green and yellow body looped and coiled through the branches of a tree. It hissed as it approached and its eyes sparkled.

"What do we do?" I gasped.

"You can run forever, but it will catch you. And no weapon can harm it. Only if you stare fearlessly into its eyes can it be destroyed."

My heart pounded as the horrid thing came closer. It spat and hissed. The human head on the snake body stretched upward. Its eyes stared into mine. I stared back, trying with all my will to show no fear. The creature began to shudder. Its mouth opened. It screamed.

121

And then it was gone.

Gwendolyn put a hand on my shoulder and her head against my chest. "Oh thank you," she cried. "You destroyed the Jebua with your courage. For this, I will always remember you."

She stood back. Her hands trembling, she slipped a tiny emerald ring from her finger. Gently, she pressed the ring into my right palm.

Speechless, I stared at her.

"I will never forget you," said Gwendolyn. "But I must leave you now." She kissed my cheek. Then, on tiny feet, she dashed away into the forest.

"Wait!" I called. But she was gone.

Suddenly the world about me turned dark. My mind became blank. My thoughts seemed to be floating—upward and outward from a dream.

I opened my eyes. I was in my bed, in my room. Morning light was streaming through the window. I could hear my father talking downstairs, and I could smell breakfast cooking.

I sat up on the edge of my bed. I kept thinking about my dream. It kept going through my head. It had all seemed so real. But, of course, that was impossible. Dreams just aren't real.

Or are they?

It was then I realized my right fist was clenched. I could feel something. For a moment I was almost afraid to look. Then I slowly opened my hand. There in my palm was a tiny emerald ring.

THINKING ABOUT WHAT YOU HAVE READ

Answer in complete sentences.

1. To which time-period does the storyteller go in his dream?

   _____

   _____

2. Who is Gwendolyn? What does she look like?

   _____

   _____

   _____

   _____

3. What does the Serpent look like? How can it be destroyed?

   _____

   _____

   _____

   _____

4. In the story there is conflict with the supernatural. Describe this conflict.

   _____

   _____

   _____

5. At the end of the story the storyteller wakes up from his dream. In his hand is a tiny emerald ring. Why is this ring important to the story?

   _____

   _____

   _____

   _____

ᗩHINKING ᗩBOUT ᗯRITING

Paragraphing a Story

In Lesson 12, you rearranged the paragraphs of a nonfiction selection. Paragraphing a short story is a little more complicated.

In a story, there are usually characters. Each time a character completes one sequence of actions, the paragraph ends and another begins. For example:

> Almost against his will, Steve took a step toward the cabin. Then another. And then he was in the cabin, walking toward the money.
> He stopped. He looked at the sleeping man. Then he looked at the bags of money. He could pick them up. He could take them and turn them over to the police.

Each time the writer of a story switches from one character to another, a new paragraph begins. For example:

> Steve stumbled out of the bushes toward them. He opened his mouth as if to say something. His head jerked to one side. His eyes opened wide with fear.
> Mary turned and looked in the direction Steve was looking. She saw the man in the sports jacket trying to pull himself over the lip of the hill. Wildly, she looked around for some route of escape.

Stories also contain dialogue—characters talking. Each time a different character speaks, a new paragraph begins. For example:

> "He must be gone now," said Mary, softly, peering up over a branch.
> "Maybe we should try making it back home now," Steve suggested.

Each paragraph in the following story is actually two paragraphs run together. By drawing boxes, divide each paragraph into two. Two paragraphs have been marked for you.

Dreams Can Come True

> Thorstein glanced at his watch again. His irritation increased. Grace Johnson, the woman from the coroner's office, had insisted she see him that afternoon about the Williams case. She had said she would be there no later than half past three. It was already a few minutes after four. Idly, Thorstein picked Williams's medical profile off his desk and flipped it open.
> Bryant Williams, 41 years old, had been admitted to City Hospital five days ago. The diagnosis had been that Williams suffered from a "sleep disorder." He was having the same type of nightmare over and over, and was afraid of going to sleep. Otherwise, the man had been in good health.

Closing the folder, Thorstein recalled Williams's description of his dreams. In them, Williams was always standing on a beach as a giant wall of sea water slowly approached him. Each night the water—the tidal wave—got closer. Finally it got so close that Williams was afraid to go to sleep. "But it's just a dream," Thorstein had reassured him.

"No, it's not, doctor," Williams had answered. "It's something real. I have a dream that's really happening." For three days the man had paced his private room in the hospital. He refused to lie down. He refused medication. He was exhausted and was losing weight.

On the night of the third day, Thorstein took matters in his own hands. He had a sleeping powder sprinkled in Williams's food. It had seemed the right thing to do. The intercom buzzed on Thorstein's desk, jarring him from his thoughts. Alvin, Thorstein's secretary, announced that Grace Johnson, from the coroner's office, had arrived.

"Sorry to have kept you waiting," a slender woman said as she entered Thorstein's office. "Quite all right," said Thorstein, emptily, pointing to a seat.

"What can you tell me about the death of Bryant Williams?" she asked, looking up from a sheaf of papers on her lap. "Sleep disorder," said Thorstein. "He refused to sleep, afraid of a recurring nightmare he'd been having. I had a sleeping powder sprinkled in his food. The next morning we found him dead."

"I have the autopsy report here," said the woman. "And, frankly, I find it baffling." "In what way?" asked Thorstein, suddenly becoming uneasy.

"Mr. Williams had sea water in his lungs." "What?" Thorstein blurted. "I don't understand."

"Neither do I," said the woman. "But the fact of the matter is that Mr. Williams died from drowning." Not knowing all the circumstances of the case, it was both startling and confusing to her when Thorstein's mouth dropped open and he began to tremble.

Getting Ready to Write

Soon you will write a short story. The following activities will help you get ready to write.

This is the basic plot of your story: you go to bed one night; you have a dream; when you wake up you find evidence that the dream was real.

This plot line is the same as that of the story "The Ring." In that story, you may recall, a boy has a dream in which he is given a ring. When he wakes up, the ring is in his hand.

The details in your story, however, should be quite different. In your story, something other than a ring will be used to show that the dream was real.

I.

Decide where you go in your dream. Underline one of the places listed below. If you prefer, write your own idea on the line.

into a desert   down a long river on a raft   into prehistoric times   on a pirate ship

into the future   into the days when Washington and his army were fighting the British

on a desert island   for a walk along the bottom of the ocean   into a mysterious cave

II.

Now think about what happens to you in your dream. What do you see? What problems do you face? How do you solve them? On a separate sheet of paper, write some of your ideas about this dream action.

III.

In your dream, you will find something, or something will be given to you, or something will happen to you that will later turn out to be proof that your dream was real. Underline the thing below that will be your proof. Or write your own idea on the line.

your feet are muddy   you have a cut   you are invisible   there is a bracelet on your wrist

you see yourself on a TV show   you have a sunburn   you are holding a piece of treasure

there is a dinosaur egg next to your bed

_____

IV.

Begin your story by telling how you had a strange dream. On a separate sheet of paper, write a rough draft of your first paragraph. Begin with something like the following: *Last night I went to bed later than usual. I had a strange dream . . .*

A Story

On a separate sheet of paper, write the story you planned in "Getting Ready to Write."

SKILL BUILDING

Quotation Marks in a Story

A direct quotation tells a person's exact words. To set off a direct quotation from the rest of a sentence, quotation marks (" ") are used.

> **EXAMPLE:**   "We know you're very strong, Robbie," said Ms. Tinker, "but
> how could even a strong guy like you carry your mom?"
> "She isn't very big," Robbie grumbled.
> "But I've met your mother. She's twice your size."

Follow these rules for using quotation marks:
1. Periods and commas that follow a quotation go inside the quotation marks.
2. Question marks and exclamation points that are part of a quotation are placed inside the quotation marks.
3. Each time a character begins to speak, the first word is capitalized.
4. When a sentence that is a direct quotation is interrupted by an expression such as *she said*, the second part of the sentence begins with a small letter.
5. Two or more sentences can be placed inside one set of quotation marks. For example:
   "But I've met your mother. She's twice your size."
   (incorrect): "But I've met your mother.✗ ✗She's twice your size."
6. Quotation marks are also placed around the titles of short stories, articles, poems, songs, and chapters of books.

The quotation marks are missing from the following story. Read the story carefully. Add the quotation marks where they belong.

The Gimmick

Elmer Loafenflabber wanted to be muscular and in good shape. But ever since he was a child he had been extremely lazy. His idea of exercise was to slowly amble to the TV set to change the station. When he rode his bike, his parents had to push him.

At the age of 40, Elmer married a woman named Fredericka. Fredericka worried about him. One day she said, Sweetums, you've got to get some exercise.

Right you are, hon, said Elmer, gasping and out of breath from so much talking.

Elmer seemed to pay no attention to his wife's advice. Deep down, though, he realized she was right. With great effort, he started looking through the ads in *Musclechunks* magazine. Suddenly his eyes lit up with joy.

Look, Fredericka, he cried. I've found the answer to my prayers. There's an ad here about Dr. Strong's clinic that says I can get into terrific shape effortlessly and quickly.

Before Fredericka could say anything, Elmer had hopped into his car and was off to Dr. Strong's clinic. He screeched to a stop in front of a very fancy and expensive-looking building.

I read your ad in a magazine, Elmer said to the receptionist. How do I get into shape and be muscular just as easily as the ad promises?

The receptionist pushed a button. Dr. Strong will see you right away, sir. Please go in.

Elmer walked into a beautifully furnished office. An athletic-looking man, dressed in a jogging suit, was seated behind a big desk.

Hi, said Elmer. I want to get into shape. I read . . .

The man smiled and handed him a bottle of red liquid. Drink this and you will have more muscles than you can imagine, said Dr. Strong.

But what does it cost? asked Elmer.

Only 20 cents, replied the man.

Elmer looked around the office. It looked very fancy. Wow, only 20 cents! said Elmer. But you look as though you're rich. How do you make any money selling your great invention for so little? he asked as he put 20 cents on the man's desk.

Dr. Strong smiled. Just take the formula, and I'll see you tomorrow, said the man.

When he got home, Elmer drank the liquid. An hour later he felt terrific. Two hours later he had rippling muscles. By bedtime he looked like a picture of a champion body-builder.

The next morning Elmer tore off the blankets and lurched out of bed. Something was wrong. He looked in the mirror. He saw a strange, muscle-bound monster! There were muscles upon muscles upon muscles. He looked horrible, ridiculous. He was so muscular he could hardly move.

Elmer, what has happened to you! Fredericka yelled. That formula turned you into a freak! You go right back to that phony doctor and demand a cure.

Less than an hour later, Elmer was in Dr. Strong's office. Your formula worked too well! Elmer cried. Now I'm too muscular. I look terrible. Now I need a formula to make me normal.

The man smiled. This is a very luxurious office, don't you think? he asked.

Yes, stammered Elmer. But that's not the point. The point is, can you make me look normal?

Strong nodded and reached into a desk drawer. He took out a bottle of blue liquid.

Will that make me normal? asked Elmer.

Yes, indeed it will.

Elmer reached for the bottle. The man closed his hand. Not so fast, he said with a smirk. What? mumbled Elmer.

The first formula cost 20 cents, said Strong. This one costs $20,000.

Elmer plopped down in a chair. Then, holding a pen in his muscular hand, he wrote out a check. As he did, the key to Dr. Strong's success slowly dawned on him.

THINKING ABOUT WRITING

1. Reread your story. Is it correctly divided into paragraphs? Are there any places where you ran two or more paragraphs together? If so, by drawing lines, show how they should be divided.

SKILL BUILDING

2. Did you use quoted dialogue in your story? If not, try rewriting it so that you have your characters talking.

3. Recheck your usage of the following punctuation marks: period, question mark, exclamation point, comma, semicolon, parentheses, dash, hyphen, quotation marks. Make any changes or corrections necessary.

4. Check for the following in your composition: fragments, incorrect pronoun case, problems in subject-verb agreement, run-ons, homophone errors. Correct any mistakes you find.

THE INTERPRETIVE ESSAY

Many times while you are in school you will read a story or a poem. You will analyze it and discuss it in class. Then you will be asked to write an interpretive essay about the work. Your essay will summarize what the story or poem is about and what it means.

Read the poem, "The Answer." Then read the model interpretive essay that follows the poem.

The Answer

A scientific type
Dr. Thurgood W. Melf
Built the biggest computer—
Did it by himself.

He would ask it the biggest question—
Yes, this he would find out:
What, oh, what is the meaning of life?
Or, what's it all about?

So in he punched his question
Got an immediate reply.
Said the computer, "What life means
Is just 4–1–7–0–5."

Melf, oh, he was puzzled
And very, very upset.
He had the answer to his question
But didn't know what it meant.

A bunch of little numbers
Simply written in a row:
Was that the meaning of life?
The doctor didn't know.

He asked the question again
And the same reply came out:
"Doctor, 4–1–7–0–5
Is what life is all about."

Then Melf had another idea.
He inquired of the machine:
"Please explain your answer.
Tell me what it means."

The computer tackled this question
That Melf to it had fed.
Shortly it gave an answer,
And this is what it said:

"You now know life's meaning—
It is 4–1–7–0–5.
But what these numbers mean
You must now decide.

"And that is the answer
My good dear Dr. Melf.
In life there are some things
You must answer for yourself."

By E. G. Dadio

An Interpretation of "The Answer"

The poem "The Answer" was written by E. G. Dadio. It is a partly serious, partly humorous poem.

In the poem, a scientist named Thurgood W. Melf builds a large computer. He asks the computer to tell him the meaning of life. The computer answers, "What life means/ Is just 4—1—7—0—5."

Melf is upset and puzzled. He has the answer to his great question about the meaning of life. The only problem is that he doesn't know the meaning of the answer.

Melf goes to the computer again. He asks it to explain the answer. He asks it to explain the meaning of the numbers 4—1—7—0—5. The computer replies that this is something Melf must figure out on his own. It tells him, "In life there are some things/ You must answer for yourself."

Thus, although the computer gives Melf the answer, the scientist has to decide for himself what the answer means. He is back to where he started. In the beginning he does not know what life is all about. And even with the answer, he still doesn't know. For Melf, the riddle of life's meaning has not been solved; it has only taken a different form.

What Melf probably learns from all of this is that there are some things that cannot be answered simply. There are some things that even a computer cannot tell you. People must find their own answers. They have to figure things out for themselves.

I like the poem "The Answer." It is funny and easy to read. More important, however, is the fact that it has a message to convey.

THINKING ABOUT WHAT YOU HAVE READ

Answer in complete sentences.

1. Do you like the poem "The Answer"? Explain.

_____

_____

_____

_____

2. What, in your opinion, is the main point the poem is trying to make?

_____

_____

_____

_____

3. Read the essay again. Does it do a good job of telling what happens in the poem? Explain.

_____

_____

_____

_____

4. The essay does more than just summarize the poem. It also interprets (explains) its meaning. In your opinion, is it a correct interpretation? Is it well written? Explain.

_____

_____

_____

_____

_____

THINKING ABOUT WRITING

Parallel Structure

Read the following sentence.

Gracie Grasstains liked to spend her free time *talking* to her pet duck, *to feed* her plastic chickens, and *swung* on vines from tree to tree.

The sentence describes three actions in a series. Each action has a different grammatical construction. The first action is *talking*, the second is *to feed*, and the third is *swung*.

The sentence can be repaired by placing the three parts in the same grammatical form. For example:

Gracie Grasstains liked to spend her free time <u>talking</u> to her pet duck, <u>feeding</u> her plastic chickens, and <u>swinging</u> on vines from tree to tree.

OR . . .

In her free time, Gracie Grasstains liked <u>to talk</u> to her pet duck, <u>to feed</u> her plastic chickens, and <u>to swing</u> on vines from tree to tree.

OR . . .

In her free time, Gracie Grasstains <u>talked</u> to her pet duck, <u>fed</u> her plastic chickens, and <u>swung</u> on vines from tree to tree.

In each example the grammar is consistent. This grammatical consistency is called *parallel structure.*

Each of the following sentences contains a series of three ideas. In each sentence, two of the three structures are parallel; one in each sentence is not. On the lines, rewrite each sentence so that all structures are parallel.

EXAMPLE: (incorrect): Her interests are *cooking, skiing,* and *to dance.*
(correct): Her interest are <u>cooking</u>, <u>skiing</u>, and <u>dancing.</u>

1. She *picked up* the snails, *putting* them in a bag, and *took* them home.

_____

_____

2. The wealthy eccentric man gets enjoyment from *going into* a fancy restaurant, *ordering* a huge meal, and then *takes* it home to his dog.

_____

_____

3. Her *beauty,* her *charm,* and *having so much intelligence* causes people to envy her.

_____

_____

4. The book discusses *how to buy* bean sprouts, *opening* the package, and *how to eat* them.

_____

_____

5. *To ride* giraffes, *talking* to armadillos, and *eating* flowers should all be against the law.

_____

_____

Getting Ready to Write

Soon you will write an interpretive essay about the famous poem "Richard Cory." The following activities will help you get ready to write.

I.

Carefully read the poem.

Richard Cory

Whenever Richard Cory went down town,
We people on the pavement looked at him:
He was a gentleman from sole to crown,
Clean favored, and imperially slim.   4

And he was always quietly arrayed,
And he was always human when he talked;
But still he fluttered pulses when he said,
"Good-morning," and he glittered when he walked.   8

And he was rich—yes, richer than a king—
And admirably schooled in every grace:
In fine, we thought that he was everything
To make us wish that we were in his place.   12

So on we worked, and waited for the light,
And went without the meat, and cursed the bread;
And Richard Cory, one calm summer night,
Went home and put a bullet through his head.   16

By Edwin Arlington Robinson

II.

On a separate sheet of paper, write a rough draft of one or two paragraphs in which you describe what happens in the poem.

The poem "Richard Cory" makes no direct statement about life; it simply relates an incident. Still, it suggests some important lessons about life and about people.

III.

Answer the following in complete sentences. Use a separate sheet of paper.

1. The poem "Richard Cory" has a surprise ending. What is this surprise?

2. Richard Cory is a mysterious person. Do you agree? Explain.

3. In the poem, the people think Richard Cory has no problems. Why do they think this?

4. Sometimes people have problems but do not show them. How does this statement relate to the poem?

5. The poem says " . . . he was everything/To make us wish that we were in his place." Why did people feel this way about Richard Cory? How do you think they felt after he killed himself?

IV.

What would you include in an introductory paragraph for an essay about the poem "Richard Cory"? In the first sentence you would give the name of the poem and its author. You would follow this with one or two sentences that make a general comment about the poem. For example, it is "interesting" or "very dramatic" or "it tells a story with a surprise ending."

On a separate sheet of paper, write a draft of the first paragraph of an essay about this poem.

An Interpretive Essay

On a separate sheet of paper, write an essay about the poem "Richard Cory." Begin with an introductory paragraph. Then write a description of what happens in the poem. Next, give your interpretation of the meaning of the poem. Add a concluding paragraph. Use your answers to "Getting Ready to Write" (pages 133–134) to help you.

SKILL BUILDING

Punctuation Review

In lessons 8 through 15, you learned about punctuation marks. The following activities will refresh your memory of where and when to use these marks.

I.

All the punctuation marks (except periods) are missing from the following sentences. The mark or marks needed in each sentence are given after each sentence. Place the punctuation marks where they belong.

1. Samuel Clemens Mark Twain was one of the first persons in the world to use a typewriter.   ( )

2. Thomas Weldon the stoop shoulder minister claims that it took 1,600 years to write the Bible.   , - ,

3. These famous women all had children after the age of 40 Lucille Ball Audrey Hepburn Gloria Vanderbilt and Rosalynn Carter.   , : , ,

4. A snake at the London Zoo said Tom was fitted with a glass eye.   " " " " , ,

5. I once read I don't remember where that a moth hears through the hairs on its body.

II.

In the following sentences there are boxes where punctuation marks should go. Read each sentence carefully, then place the correct punctuation mark in each box. (Some punctuation marks are already given.)
   In some sentences, more than one type of mark may be correct. In these cases, choose the mark *you* feel is best. Be prepared to explain why you chose it over the others.

1. "Did the idea of eating with a fork come from the Orient ☐ " she asked ☐

2. Women in ancient Peru wore lipstick ☐ they also darkened their eyebrows with black grease paint.

3. I think ☐ no, I'm sure ☐ the book said that the people of Finland used to put windows in their coffins.

4. The following are names of cities in Canada ☐ London ☐ Kitchener ☐ and Surrey.

5. "High heels [ ] " said Mary [ ] "were first worn by ancient kings who were not allowed to touch their heels to the ground."

6. The Aymaras [ ] a tribe of Indians in South America [ ] believe that eating too many sweets causes a worm to grow in the stomach [ ] and that the worm causes hiccups.

7. "The Roman Emperor Heliogabalus [ ] third century [ ] slept on a bed of solid silver [ ] " said Mr. Dale [ ] my history teacher.

8. When glasses were invented in the sixteenth century [ ] doctors warned people not to use them [ ] they believed poor vision should be treated with ointments rubbed on the eyes.

9. Goggles [ ] however [ ] were invented by the Eskimos.

10. [ ] It is known, [ ] she said, [ ] that northern Germans wore fingerless gloves in the eighth and ninth centuries. [ ]

WRITING RECHECK

THINKING ABOUT WRITING

1. Reread your interpretive essay. Are there any cases where your sentence structures are not parallel? If so, correct any errors you find.

2. Did you give your essay a title? If not, do so now.

3. Exchange essays with a classmate. Are there important facts or ideas brought out in your classmate's paper that you should have included in yours? If so, on your own paper, make a list of things that would improve your essay.

SKILL BUILDING

4. In your essay, did you quote any lines from the poem "Richard Cory"? Did you put quotation marks around the quoted lines? If you did not, do so now.

5. Recheck your usage of the following punctuation marks: period, question mark, exclamation point, comma, semicolon, parentheses, dash, hyphen, quotation marks. Make any changes or corrections necessary.

6. Check for the following in your composition: fragments, incorrect pronoun case, problems in subject-verb agreement, run-ons, homophone errors. Correct any mistakes you find.

17

IN A WORD: WRITING

In the previous lessons of this book, you completed many different writing activities. You wrote paragraphs, news stories, letters, poems, stories, plays, cartoons, and essays.

In the process, you may have discovered that you have a talent for one or two specific forms of writing. For example, you may be particularly good at writing stories and poems.

You may also have discovered how easy and enjoyable writing can be. In fact, an idea for a piece of writing can come from anywhere, even from a simple word—a word such as *water.*

Read the following selections. They are examples of different forms of writing: a news story, a fictional story, a poem, and a non-fiction piece. But the idea for each selection came from one word—*water.*

BROKEN PIPE FLOODS MERCER'S HOME

By Linda Mercer

Dallas, Texas—Last Tuesday night, three rooms of the home of Julie and Linda Mercer were flooded. The cause of the flood was a bathroom pipe that burst while the Mercers slept.

"I woke up and heard the sound of rushing water," Julie Mercer said. "As I reached the bathroom I found myself ankle-deep in water."

Julie immediately awoke her daughter, Linda. After some frantic searching, the women found the water shut-off valve.

They spent the rest of the night cleaning up. Wet rugs were thrown outside onto a patio. Then, with mops and brooms, the Mercers soaked up or swept out most of the water.

There was some damage to the floors and furniture. The Mercer home is insured against flooding.

Surf's Up!

By Don Lockwood

Many millions of years ago there were no seas or oceans on Earth. The ocean beds were huge stretches of sandy land. The fish had legs then, and they walked—instead of swam.

This all changed in the year 15922 B.C. In that year a spaceship from the planet Hangten flew to Earth. The Hangtenians were on vacation, and they were looking forward to a good time. They were especially looking forward to surfing, which was the favorite sport of the Hangtenians. They had brought their own surfboards.

But when the Hangtenians landed, they were disappointed. Earth had no oceans. And without oceans there was no surf. And without surf they couldn't go surfing!

The Hangtenians were ready to pack up their boards and head for home. But then Wallox, the chief scientist on board the spaceship, had an idea. He took one cup of turbofluid and mixed in two pinches of bubbleoxide and nine pinches of aquasalinocarbofoamo. Then he took a container of the mixture outside and set it down on the dry sand.

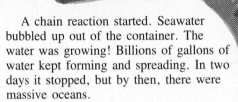

A chain reaction started. Seawater bubbled up out of the container. The water was growing! Billions of gallons of water kept forming and spreading. In two days it stopped, but by then, there were massive oceans.

The Hangtenians stayed on Earth for ten Ugas (about a year and a half), surfing every day. Finally their vacation was over, and they had to return home.

Of course, they left the oceans behind. These are the same oceans we see on Earth today. And the only reason they are there is because some visitors from outer space happened to like surfing.

At Play

It rained yesterday,
leaving
behind a vacant lot
that
has turned
into a miniature lake.
Through it
a little boy tromps,
soaking his pants and
shoes and
socks
and having a
wonderful time.
By Pamela May

What would happen if all the water in the oceans dried up? The main thing you would see would be salt. There would be four and a half cubic miles of it. This would be enough salt to cover the entire United States with a layer one and one half miles deep!

Collette Holly

THINKING ABOUT WHAT YOU HAVE READ

Answer in complete sentences.

1. Which of the pieces of writing do you like best? Explain.

   _____

   _____

   _____

2. Which selection is purely fictional? Is the tone serious or humorous? Explain.

   _____

   _____

   _____

   _____

3. Which selection is based on personal experience? What clues do you have that it is based on personal experience?

   _____

   _____

   _____

4. The paragraph about the amount of salt in the ocean is factual. What facts did you learn from this piece of writing?

   _____

   _____

   _____

5. Imagine you are a cartoonist. You are given the job of turning one of the selections on pages 137 and 138 into a cartoon. Which would you choose? Why?

   _____

   _____

Thinking About Writing

Review and Application

In previous "Thinking about Writing" activities you studied such writing techniques as paragraphing, using figurative language, and keeping sentence structure parallel. Meanwhile, in the "Skill Building" activities you encountered such writing mechanics as capitalization, punctuation, and subject-verb agreement.

In this lesson, "Thinking about Writing" and "Skill Building" have been combined. This has been done in order to help you apply the techniques and the mechanics at the same time. For example, when you write a paragraph, you must think about such basic things as punctuation as well as the form and content of the paragraph.

There are many errors in the following story. Make all the necessary changes and corrections by writing between the lines. One change has been done for you.

The Room

Edward Deele pulled the black-and-white car two a crackling halt in the gravel driveway in front of

the old Crooms place a teenage girl, her face a mask of fear, trembled.

"Their gone. It's all my fault" whined the girl as Deele came closer and approached, dro

pping his baton into the loop on his belt.

"Take it easy. What happened"?

"I called you—the police. I didn't know what to do something happens in that house, that room

up there." Deele peeked up at the sagging two story house it been built by Elias Crooms, with him

own hands, in the '60s. Recently, Crooms and his wife had disappeared. Although foul play was

suspected, no charge was brought against anyone.

"Alaria; my name is Andrea Alaria. We were out driving. I dared my brother Rudy and his friend

Jack that they couldn't stay in Crooms's house overnight. They said they could. We entered the

house at about 12 30 or so. Jack and rudy climbed and went up these stairs. i heard screams, and

then they just disappeared. Deele smiled. "Listen," he said, "their trying to scare you."

"Well, I'll just have to go in and get they, won't I" said Deele as he walked to the front door. With one hand, he was pulling a splintering bored off the doorway, pried off another with his baton. He gave the door a hefty kick, it sprang open. He found himself in a dark, moldering hallway.

"Alright, guys, he called out as he reached the foot of the stairwell. "Game's over. Come out."

He paused for not really a very long time, then made his way up the warped creaking stares. At the top of the stairs there were a single solitary door. Suddenly uneasy, he slowly opened it, his mind flooding with a vision of two boys lying dead. Perhaps there been a killer in the house. was he still there—in the room—watching and waited to strike again. Coming up the stairs had frighte ned Deele.

But the room was empty. There was no killer. But something was wrong.

He looked around. There were a few odds-and-ends of furniture an upturned night table, a three legged chair, a broken down dresser and a chipped mirror. Something about the mirror attra cted deele's attention. He wondering what it was him saw—wondered what it were he didn't see.

he looked down, saw nothing he screamed, then screamed again. He looked in the mirr or—and saw nothing.

Getting Ready to Write

Your final writing activity in this book will be based on the word *automobile,*
using a format of your choice. The following activities will help you get ready
to write. Write your answers on a separate sheet of paper.

1. Imagine you are going to write a personal narrative based on an experience with a car. In one or two sentences, describe the incident about which you'd write your narrative.

2. Now imagine you are going to turn this personal experience involving an automobile into a newspaper story. Write the opening (or *lead*) paragraph. (To refresh your memory about newspaper writing, refer to lesson 5.)

3. Imagine you are writing a business letter to the following person: Mr. Nathan Studebaker, the curator of the Museum of Automobile History. The address is 283746 Exhaust Ave., New York, NY 10027.
   You are the owner of a 1940 Crosley, in mint condition. You wish to sell it for $20,000.
   Write the heading, inside address, and salutation for such a business letter. (To refresh your memory about writing a business letter, refer to lesson 11.)

4. Imagine you want to write a three sentence paragraph about the invention of the automobile. Name some of the places where you might find this information.

5. Imagine you want to write a story in which a car plays an important role. Why is the car important? Does anything exciting happen to the person driving it? Describe a plot idea for a story inspired by the word *automobile*.

Your Choice

Use the word *automobile* as the basis for your writing. Choose one of the following forms: personal narrative, news story, business letter, three-sentence paragraph, short story, objective poem, or play. Use your answers to "Getting Ready to Write" to help you. You may also wish to look back at the models on pages 137 and 138.

1. On the following lines, list the punctuation and mechanics errors you should look for in your own writing. Try not to look back at the earlier lessons in the book.

_____

_____

_____

_____

_____

2. Now, look back at earlier "Writing Recheck" activities. If you find anything missing from your list, add it on the lines above.

3. Reread the writing you did for this lesson. Make any necessary changes or corrections.